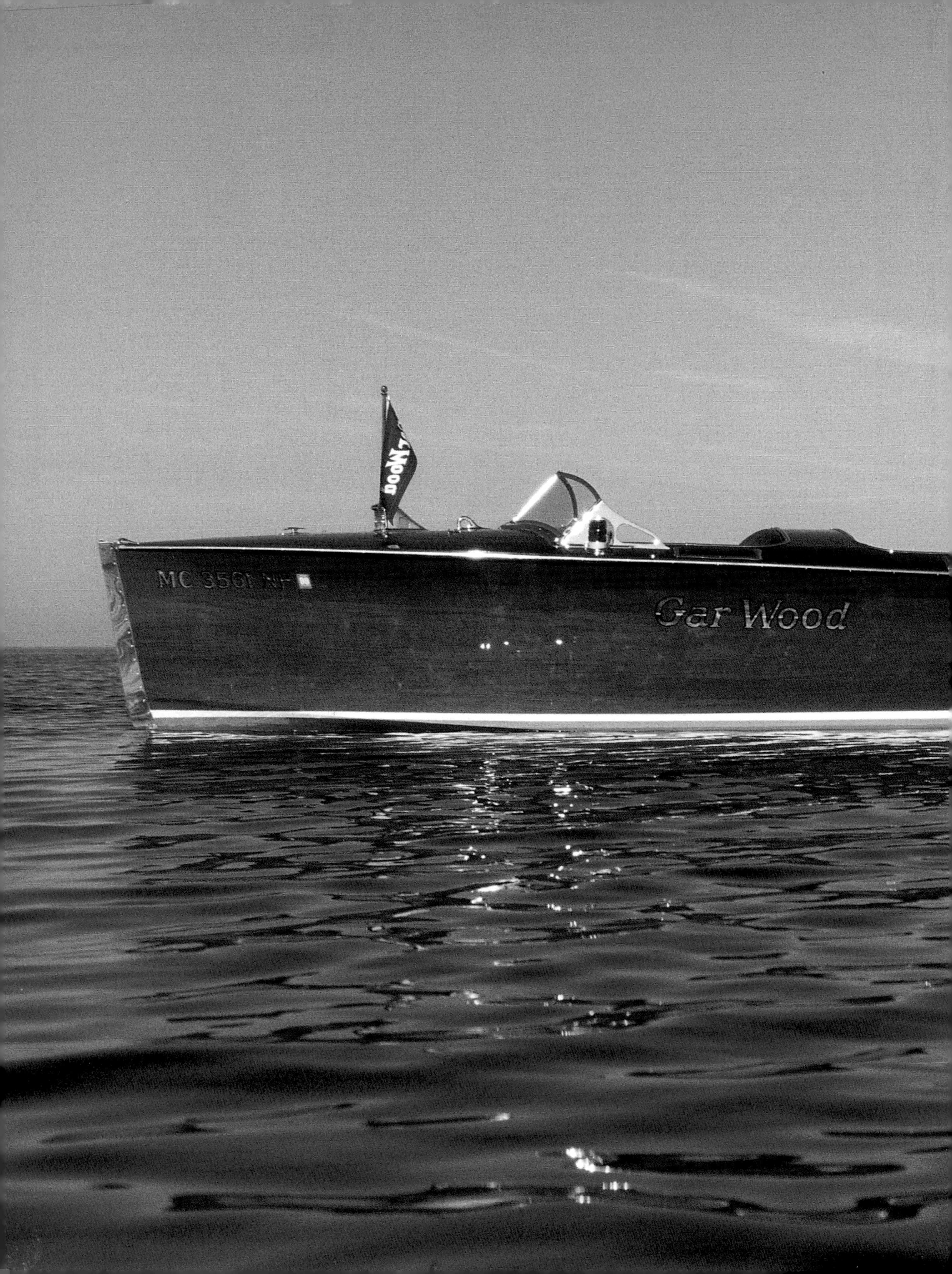
MC 3561 NF
Gar Wood

Gar Wood
BOATS
Classics of a Golden Era

Anthony S. Mollica Jr.

MBI Publishing Company

Dedication

To my father

who introduced me to the elegance of Gar Wood Boats. His confidence gave me the opportunity to be fully responsible for the operation and care of the family Gar Wood from the time I was 13 years old. The lessons I learned through his trust in me influenced much in my life and strengthened my appreciation for his wisdom.

And to Elizabeth, my dear wife,

who encouraged me 22 years ago to search for the old family Gar Wood and to rekindle a childhood passion. It was her reassuring support that provided the spirit for me to continue searching for material in preparation of this book.
—Anthony S. Mollica Jr.

Acknowledgments

I wish to thank the scores of people who contributed to this significant story. It could not have been completed without considerable help. Their willingness to share memories, photographs, and documents provided me the special privilege of preparing this book for all who enjoy the history of great classic boats.

Fred Alter, Jeff Beard, Charles Beattie, Conrad Berger, Joan Brack, Jim Brennan, Jim Brown, Catherine Lisee Burns, Ralph Bush, John Clark, Robert Cox, Thomas Crew, Lewis Crosley, Richard Curley, William Danforth, Roy Dryer, John Dubickas, Bruce Duncan, William Feikert, Thomas Frauenheim, William Gage, Brian Gagnon, Fred Genaw, Joseph Gribbens, Dean Guy, Nat Hammond, Rebecca Hopfinger, Richard Hopgood, Lindsey Hopkins, Tony Hyman, Robert Joachim, Chris Johnson, Victor Johnson, Tom Juul, Elmer Kadar, James Lane, William Lester, Carl Lisee, Clara Lisee, Robert Mack, Craig Magnuson, Elizabeth Magri, Jack Magri, Alan Mann, Don Mayea, Larry Mayea, Edward Mehrmann, Tom Mendenhall, John Morrison, Elizabeth Murray, Robert Neal, William Northup, Fred Patterson, Edward Posey, Don Price, Jeffrey Rodengen, James Rodgers, Arnie Rubenstein, Jack Savage, Dennis Schauer, Al Schinnerer, Bert Self, Victoria Sharps, Francis Shepardson, William Siegenthaler, Thomas Simmons, Don Smither, Lou Smith, Martin Smith, Robert Smith, Kenneth Spalding, Robert Speltz, Ella Stewart, Joyce Lisee Street, David Taylor, Larry Taylor, Dan Teetor, Jack Teetor, Phoebe Tritton, Larry Turcotte, Thomas Turcotte, Anders Vaerneus, Francis VanDeVelde, Addison Vars III, Paul Walker, James Wangard, Norm Wangard, Steve Wilke, Bill Wood, Gar Wood Jr., John Worthy, William Wright, and Mark Zilm

First published in 1999 by MBI Publishing Company, 729 Prospect Avenue, PO Box 1, Osceola, WI 54020-0001 USA

© Anthony Mollica, 1999

MBI Publishing Company books are also available at discounts in bulk quantity for industrial or sales-promotional use. For details write to Special Sales Manager at Motorbooks International Wholesalers & Distributors, 729 Prospect Avenue, Osceola, WI 54020-0001 USA.

Library of Congress Cataloging-in-Publication Data
Mollica, Anthony
  Gar Wood boats : power classics of a golden era/Anthony Mollica.
      p.   cm.
  Includes Index.
  ISBN 0-7603-0607--9 (hardbound : alk. paper) 1. Motorbooks—United States. 2. Wood Garfield Arthur, 1880—Contributions in boatbuilding. 3. Boatbuilding—United States. I. Title.
  VM341.M65   1999
  623.8'231'092—dc21   99-12437

On the front cover: The twin-engined, 24-foot, 6-inch custom utility *Leading Lady*, shown here speeding across Lake Tahoe, was featured in Gar Wood's display at the 1940 New York Boat Show. *Classic Boating*

On the frontispiece: The handsome bow treatment of this 22-foot custom runabout is a fine example of Gar Wood's elegant styling of the late 1930s. *Classic Boating*

On the title page: The 28-foot triple cockpit "Seemego" is a wonderful example of the design that elevated Gar Wood's styling above all its rivals. *Dan Teetor*

On the back cover: Top: The "Gar Sr.," Gar Wood's 70-foot personal yacht, was transformed many times to suit his boating needs by Nap Lisee's expert carpenters. *Gar Wood photo* Bottom: The "Maggie B" is one of the rare 1940 28-foot runabouts powered by a 316-horsepower V-12 Scripps engine with a top speed of 46 miles per hour. *Bill Gage photo*

Edited by Paul Johnson
Designed by Rebecca Allen

Printed in Hong Kong

Contents

Preface

Fifty-three years ago I was painting the bilge of our family Gar Wood and wondered if anyone would ever appreciate how skillfully I was performing my task. As I continued my work I dreamed that in some telepathic way Gar Wood, himself, would declare our boat to be the very best maintained Gar Wood in the world. It was a time before there were classic boat shows with teams of expert judges and long before our sleek boat would be called an antique. On that hot summer's day all I wanted was someone to appreciate the value of a clean, perfectly painted bilge.

In 1938 a business associate of my father traded his 25-foot Chris-Craft Clipper Cruiser for a new 32-foot Chris-Craft semi-enclosed cruiser. I was six years old at the time and thought it was the most beautiful boat that I could imagine. I drew sketches of this boat at home and at school. The following year, he traded it for a new 41-foot double-cabin enclosed bridge Chris-Craft, which was even more beautiful. I was starstruck! For me, cruising in a big, new Chris-Craft had to be the best life could offer. From that time on, my free thoughts simply drifted automatically toward Chris-Craft boats.

One day my father brought home the 1941 Show Issue of *Motor Boating* magazine. I probably thumbed through it hundreds of times, reading the same ads and absorbing each picture. As much as I admired Chris-Crafts, I was captivated by the illustrations of the Gar Wood Boats and soon they became my vision of design perfection.

As World War II drew to a close my father located a boat that had been in storage during most of the war years. The boat was a nearly new 1941 Gar Wood "Vacationer" model. After due consideration, he decided to buy it. His decision and this boat had a profound influence on our family activities for many years.

The family Gar Wood became a significant influence in my life. Its care and maintenance helped me acquire new skills for refinishing, woodworking, engine work, seasonal lay-up, and fitting out in the spring.

I became interested in knowing more about Gar Wood Boats and the man who founded the company. I began collecting brochures, articles, and stories related to Gar Wood Boats. In the winter of 1947 my father surprised me with news that we were going to New York City for the National Motor Boat Show where the new Gar Woods would be on display. It was an important event in my life. Just a few months later, in the summer of that year, we read that the Gar Wood Boat factory had closed.

Other events, such as college, marriage, and work, established new priorities in my life, and my father's decision to sell the family Gar Wood didn't hit me with full impact. When the day arrived to transfer our Gar Wood to the new owner, however, I wasn't so sure it was the right thing to do. I quietly made a personal commitment at that moment that someday, when the time was right, I would own a Gar Wood once more.

It was nearly 20 years before I was in a position to own another Gar Wood, which was 30 years since Gar Wood built its last boat in 1947. Finding a good one could be a challenge. In 1978 providence intervened when I read a classified ad in *Hemmings Motor News*—someone in North Carolina was selling a Gar Wood that had been in storage for 28 years. It was similar to our family's original Gar Wood, with an identical Chrysler Crown engine.

Bringing home the Gar Wood was an exciting time, and my children wanted to be involved in the activities to get the boat back in top shape. All we needed was some information regarding original equipment, the proper color stain, step pads, and some hardware. My experience restoring old cars led me to believe that I could simply contact the national Gar Wood owners' association for information.

I was not prepared to learn that there was no such organization. I was completely on my own to try to find original Gar Wood parts. Suddenly I had taken on two tasks: restoring my Gar Wood and establishing an international organization of Gar Wood owners.

In 1979 I founded the Gar Wood Society to help Gar Wood owners, like me, to maintain their boats to original factory specifications. The volumes of research collected in this effort over the past 20 years can now provide a more detailed picture of the Gar Wood operation never presented before.

The story of Gar Wood Boats is a fascinating tale of achievement in sports and industry. It's the story of a remarkable man who was a successful inventor and a corporate executive. He amassed a personal fortune in excess of $50 million before 1940. His skill at speedboat racing was beyond all competition, resulting in total domination of the sport for nearly 20 years. Gar Wood not only drove the boats to victory, he designed and built them in his own shops. When boat competition lagged, he challenged the fastest express trains in North America and won every time. He independently challenged all the industrial nations of the world to build and operate an unlimited speedboat that could beat him. Seven times in 13 years three nations tried, but none could do it.

His inventions can still be found on modern electric golf carts, passenger aircraft, and modern cruise ships. His popular speedboats, the subject of this book, are considered to be the most sought-after classic boats in the world.

—*Anthony S. Mollica Jr.*

Introduction

Boatbuilding has always been a perilous business. Success for more than a brief time often requires many elements beyond good designs, skilled craftsmen, and abundant resources. Sometimes it is equally important to have a keen sense of timing and a measure of good luck.

Many of the most exciting boats of the golden era were in production for only a brief period when compared to other industries of their time. Some of the boatbuilding companies closed at puzzling times when boats were in demand and the national economy seemed solid. Other boatbuilders were so marginal that even the slightest economic downturn was enough to end their production. The Great Depression following the 1929 stock market crash was particularly cruel to boatbuilders.

Established boatbuilding firms that were unable to maintain their sales and production operations through the post-Depression years included such wonderful classics as Robinson Seagull, Dodge Watercar, Sea Lyon, Belle Isle Bearcat, Dawn, ACF, Mullins, Dart, Albany, and Ditchburn. Today these boats are among the most sought-after names by boat collectors because of their superior design, outstanding performance, and, of course, rarity.

The post-Depression period so devastating for most boatbuilders turned out to be peak years in Gar Wood's racing career. In 1931 his *Miss America IX* became the first boat to exceed 100 miles per hour. Over the next 18 months he improved on that particular record four times, each one an official new world record. On September 20, 1932, his ultimate *Miss America*, the Tenth in the series, set a 1-mile speed record of 124.9 miles per hour that would stand for years. In an economically depressed world, Gar Wood was still a champion without equal.

When Gar Wood's pleasure boat sales slipped to their lowest volume ever, his vast personal wealth and his successful hoist business maintained the boat factory's activity. He told his designers it was time to develop a new line of smaller, less expensive boats to meet the challenges of the weaker market without compromising Gar Wood's established reputation for superior quality.

Gar Wood's boat company was always a source of personal pride for him. He insisted on standards of excellence that were unique in the boatbuilding industry and resulted in the finest standardized boats of their time. He personally approved and tested every new design before it went into production. His boat carpenters were the best in the trade and fiercely loyal to Wood.

Surprisingly, the Gar Wood Boat Company had its genesis in decisions made by people other than Gar Wood.

This, in itself, is quite remarkable because Wood had a reputation for always being in control of his own destiny.

The story of Gar Wood is one of the most compelling tales of achievement of any American sports champion. He individually challenged the nations of the world to build a faster boat than his and then try to beat him. Each national team that tried failed. His achievements and records have endured for decades and some still stand. He was an accomplished inventor who at one time held more industrial patents than any other living American.

As chance would have it, his unplanned experience in the boatbuilding business may turn out to be his most enduring legacy. All of Gar Wood's industrial operations have been renamed or sold, and his speed records are being eclipsed by modern challengers. Yet his pleasure boats have become the most sought-after classics among contemporary collectors throughout the world. It was Gar Wood's insistence on uncompromising quality, superior design, and outstanding performance that attracts the interest of classic boat collectors around the world.

Gar Wood Boats, Classics of a Golden Era is the long-awaited story behind these remarkable boats that bear the name of the world's greatest speedboat champion. It's the detailed account of every standard Gar Wood production model as well as their better known custom designs. Much of the information in this book has never been published in any form, and it contains many unusual photographs from Gar Wood's personal collection.

GAR WOOD TERMINOLOGY FOR SPECIAL MODELS

Baby Gar: the original 33-foot gentleman's runabout and production model from 1922 to 1929

Baby Gar Jr.: a 26-foot production runabout/sedan built only in 1927

Baby Gar 28: the early raised-deck production model of the 28-foot runabout/sedan, 1927 to 1929

Gar Jr.: the original express cruiser design, 1918 to 1920, usually 36 feet

Gar Jr. II: 50-foot express cruiser known as the Flyer; six to eight built with custom cabin designs

Gar Sr.: the name given to the 70-foot Cigarette after it was repurchased from Hamersley in 1925

Garfield A. Wood

Inventor and Industrialist

The magnificent 70-foot *Gar Sr.* express cruiser was originally built for Gordon Hammersley by Gar Wood. It is powered by five Liberty engines and was named *Cigarette*. In 1925 Wood redesigned and named it *Gar Sr.* It became his personal yacht for more than 20 years.
Mystic Seaport, Rosenfeld Collection, Mystic, Connecticut

It was called the "tremendous '20s." It was an age of great champions, extraordinary events, superb performances, and a time of remarkable public heroes. Never before had there been such a concentration of outstanding champions in so many fields of sport.

The decade arrived along with prosperity and a score of great sports writers to record the exploits of these champions who established records that have endured and are still heralded. Today the equipment is better, the rules are different, and the games have changed; but it cannot be disputed that the great performances of the "tremendous '20s" stood out from their predecessors to a greater extent than did those of any other period. In golf there was Bobby Jones, tennis had Bill Tilden, in boxing there was Jack Dempsey, horse racing had the great Man O' War, the Yankees had Ruth and Gehrig, and speed-boat racing had Gar Wood who, alone, attracted the largest gatherings of spectators in the history of American sports.

America of the 1920s craved excitement and good times. The Great War in Europe was over. It was the time of the flapper, the roadster, bootleggers, boom and bust. Motorboating was becoming the new pastime of the well-to-do, and by the end of the decade more than one million Americans owned pleasure boats.

Speed and power became paramount. The passion for speed was fueled by Prohibition. Smugglers needed fast boats to avoid arrest, and the authorities needed faster boats to apprehend them. Fast yachts called "commuters" ferried investment brokers from their homes on Long Island and Connecticut to downtown Manhattan. Garfield Wood was the world's undisputed speedboat king, and everyone who could afford one wanted a Gar Wood speedboat of his own.

The Gar Wood story begins in 1880 when Elizabeth Wood gave birth to her third child, a son. Staunch Iowa Republicans, Elizabeth and Walter Wood named him after the successful Republican presidential ticket of James Garfield and Chester Arthur. James Garfield was the last of the "log cabin" presidents and a true rags-to-riches hero. The boy was named Garfield Arthur Wood, and before he reached the age of 40 "Gar" would be better known than the men for whom he was named. When Gar was 10 years old, the Wood family moved to Minnesota where his father became captain of a ferryboat near Minneapolis. Young Gar idolized his father and was in awe of his skill at piloting such a large boat. On one particular day, Captain Wood had Gar on board to help as his crew when a rival ferryboat was about to pass them. Gar Wood tells this memorable story in his own way:

In 1920 this close and successful family arranged a formal family portrait with their mother. Standing, from left: Gar, George, Harvey, Clinton, Winfield, Logan, and Lewis. Front, from left: Dorothy, Edward, Elizabeth (mother), Phil, Esther, and Bess.

The first boat race I ever took part in was on Lake Osakis. My father operated a ferry on that lake, and we had some great old times with it. Our ferry was named the *Manitoba* and its only rival was the *Merry Mann*, owned and run by old Wes Mann. Wes wouldn't give up the idea that his ferryboat, which was a wood burner, like ours, was the faster of the two, and that someday he would catch Dad unawares and prove it.

On one memorable trip across the lake, Wes caught us short of wood! His old boat was pushing us hard because we couldn't feed ours enough fuel.

"Why don't you row that old tub in?" he jeered at us as he edged alongside. "I'm passin' you standing still!"

"Blast his hide!" roared Dad. "Hey, you lads, give us a hand with this furniture! Bust her up and shove her into the firebox! We'll beat that old pirate if we have to tear up the deck!"

So we fed the fire with the chairs and tables, and, though old Wes pushed his boat for all she was worth, we beat him fair and square! I was only a kid then, but I still feel the thrill of winning that race. Right then I resolved that someday I was going to build race boats of my own.

Gar Wood retold this story countless times and confessed that each time he told it, he could still feel the thrill of winning that race to the cheering of the passengers. It may have been the imprint of that single event that influenced the course of his life. At that moment, on an old steam-driven ferry, Gar Wood's compulsion for speedboat racing began, and his remarkable success changed speedboat racing forever.

Elizabeth and Walter Wood provided Gar with eight brothers and three sisters. As a member of a large and spirited family it's not surprising that Gar grew up to be resourceful, enterprising, and self-assured. As a youth he learned to delegate instructions precisely to those who needed direction at home or at work. He was adventuresome but always well prepared for all eventualities. He took family responsibilities seriously and in time would provide employment opportunities for his entire family.

Even before he reached his teen years, Gar displayed remarkable understanding for boats and various types of engines and motors. When his father secured a coveted position as captain of a large Great Lakes freighter, the Wood family moved to Duluth. Gar promptly got a government engineering department job running the first gasoline engine launch in Duluth Harbor. While on this job he designed and built what could have been the first downdraft carburetor, enabling him to outperform all other inspection boats with bursts of phenomenal speed. It was in Duluth he also began building small boats and launches for local fishermen.

In school Gar was a bright and eager student who completed his formal education at the Armour College of Technology in Chicago. It was at Armour Tech that he refined his engineering skills and sharpened his creative talents to proceed into any mechanical challenge with the confidence that he could find the appropriate solution. It was at Armour Tech that he realized his talent in engineering often exceeded that of his instructors, which prompted him to eagerly explore employment opportunities rather than continue his college studies.

In rapid succession Wood sold lightning rods to farmers, taught automotive engineering, and became a Ford auto dealer. As a Ford dealer he sold 10 cars in his first year but was forced to close down because of lagging deliveries. In a bold act he decided to sue the Ford district distributor for the slow deliveries and won the court case. The distributor, impressed with Wood's self-confidence and assertiveness, offered him a responsible position with his automobile distribution firm.

In 1910 Gar Wood married Murlen Fellows of Duluth, the daughter of two osteopathic physicians. Murlen graduated from the University of Minnesota where she was an honor student and elected to Phi Beta Kappa. Years later Murlen told reporters that she was so taken by Gar's creativity and resourcefulness that she knew immediately that their marriage would result in an exciting future for both of them. As it turned out that exciting future began even faster than she ever imagined.

Murlen taught school while Gar operated his own machine shop, known as the G.A. Wood Company, in which he could build or fix almost anything. In 1911 he was commissioned to build a race boat named *Leading Lady* for a new customer. Wood and the boat owner, W. P. Cleveland, took the finished boat to the Mississippi Valley Powerboat Association Regatta where they competed against the fastest boats in the region. They won in style and created quite a sensation by averaging better than 31 miles per hour over the 10-mile course. This was a remarkable performance at the time and the news of Wood's obvious talent for speed in boat racing spread quickly throughout the Mississippi Valley.

It was later that year that a chance event would change everything for the young married couple. Gar and Murlen were on a street corner in St. Paul when they observed two burly men laboriously turning a hand crank to raise the bed of a fully loaded coal truck. As the men struggled and cursed at the weight of the load and the effort required, Wood became convinced that he could engineer a better way to accomplish this task. He shared his ideas with Murlen and together they agreed to invest their modest savings toward building a prototype device. Gar's idea was to eliminate the hand crank entirely and focus his thoughts on a cylindrical lift powered by hydraulics.

His first plan was to design something simple and foolproof that could be operated by the push of a button. He remembered the hydraulic cylinder on the old ferry *Manitoba* that his father used to reverse the engine. Wood told an old friend some years later, "That old cylinder was the basis of the idea and a gear pump was the other most important factor." Once again the strong relationship with his father and their activities together provided a powerful influence in his life.

He fabricated a simple device from a 54-by-5-inch cylinder and a junkyard pump salvaged from an old Buick. When it was ready he persuaded the owner of the same coal truck he observed to let him borrow the truck long enough to install his new device so he could provide a real test. When the installation was completed he gathered the coal truck owner and some of his friends who were just returning from a dinner party. The owner suggested that the truck should have weight in the dump bed to make the demonstration valid. So the owner and his friends climbed into the truck bed to lend reality to the test. Wood briefly described his system, then activated the device and promptly dumped the well-dressed cargo onto the warehouse floor. The lift worked exactly as Wood predicted. Although surprised by the quickness of the operation, no one was hurt. The truck owner was impressed and his friends remained in good humor as they dusted themselves off. The owner ordered enough of Wood's lifts for each of his coal trucks, and a prosperous new industry was about to be born.

It was a remarkable era for American industry and product development. Sound movies, tungsten light bulb filaments, variable transmissions, and seaplanes were all introduced in 1910. A year later Carrier developed air conditioning, and within five years American industries were producing refrigerators, electric hand drills, gearboxes, and the automatic pilot. It was a brilliant time for inventors. Gar Wood's hydraulic lift was recognized as one of the most significant new products of its time. It revolutionized the hauling and unloading of loose materials that could easily be dumped. The introduction of the hydraulic lift coincided with the rapid growth of heavy equipment, trucking, and so many military applications.

It was Wood, himself, who clearly understood the potential magnitude of his invention and acted quickly and precisely by protecting what he had designed. He went to a lawyer but received scant encouragement. Fortunately the lawyer's assistant overheard the conversation and, speaking to Wood about it later, made out the papers for which the patent was granted. Wood skillfully prepared an iron-clad patent description of "every nut and bolt" of his invention. The simplicity of his new hydraulic hoist and its general adaptability to any type of truck caused it to jump into immediate favor with the truck manufacturers. This is where his technical skill and mechanical knowledge paid off again by securing the rights to his application and thus protecting it from industrial theft by other well-established manufacturers. Wood used a column of oil forced into a cylinder by a pump operating from the transmission to lift the body. In addition his natural resourcefulness fought off the temptation to license other fabricators or subcontractors so that total control of production and quality was in his hands. These timely decisions would result in securing the maximum potential profit from his invention in the years ahead.

Demand for Wood's hydraulic lift out grew his limited manufacturing facilities. Pressure to expand was increasing daily and faster than his resources could handle. To solve this crisis Wood made a decision that was against his better judgment and one that he would regret for years. To raise expansion capital he sold half his interest in the hoist patent to a Minneapolis auto dealer for $5,000.

Wood was uncomfortable with his new partner from the start. The partner situation prompted him to move his operation to Detroit to be closer to the truck manufacturers, and distancing himself from his associate was his next decision. It was a wise and timely move. He quickly located new facilities that could easily accommodate the increased volume. He encouraged his brothers to consider coming into his rapidly growing business. With the trusted involvement of his brothers, Logan, Lewis, Philip, Clinton, and Harvey, he was able to move carefully from one order to the next, being cautious not to expand too quickly. Rapid expansion might expose the business to the need for another loan that could pry control of the hoist from his hands. Under his careful guidance his enterprise thrived and grew.

The early lifts were custom jobs that buyers, mostly truck manufacturers, could not easily fit into their production lines. The intricate nature of these custom applications kept Wood in control as the business grew. His Detroit factory was ideally located to supply truck manufacturers, and America's eventual involvement in World War I opened vast new applications for his invention. During the war, the Allied Forces used 3,000 Wood hoists on American-made trucks, principally to make and repair roads in the war zone. With a Wood hydraulic hoist in operation the trucks could discharge their loads quickly and get out of harm's way rapidly because they could deposit their loads in 13 seconds.

The business was a bonanza and literally lifted Wood into a financial position that enabled him to give wider attention to the boating sport and pursue his hobby without restrictions. Wood, shrewdly anticipating a weaker postwar market for the military applications of his hoist, bought out his major competitor. This acquisition also included several valuable new patents that would apply successfully to the civilian commercial truck market.

This amazing photograph of a Wood-equipped dump truck demonstrates the lifting power of the Wood hydraulic device with 18 men in the truck's cargo bed. The photo was taken in 1913 in front of the first Gar Wood factory. *Gar Wood*

In spite of his success, Wood still had an unwanted partner resulting from the $5,000 loan he needed to get his business started in St. Paul, Minnesota. It was not until 1931 that he was finally able to persuade his partner to relinquish the other half of the original hoist patent. The buyout cost Gar Wood $750,000 and forever made him wary of outside involvement in his business ventures. This painful lesson only served to increase his fierce desire to always be in control of the situation, whatever it may be.

By 1916 Wood's lifelong passion for speedboat racing could no longer be contained. As chance would have it, the association that sponsored the 1915 winning Gold Cup race boat, *Miss Detroit*, was having a luncheon meeting in downtown Detroit. The reason for the meeting was to resolve the long overdue debt to the boatbuilder. Although *Miss Detroit* was the reigning champion, her hull was battered from the previous year's races and she was no longer competitive. Chris Smith, the builder, had not been given the final payment due on the boat. The plan was to resolve the debt by offering *Miss Detroit* to the highest bidder that afternoon during the luncheon. Many of the businessmen in attendance were there simply out of curiosity to see who might emerge as the courageous high bidder.

Lee Barrett, who was head of Detroit's Bureau of Conventions and Tourism, was appointed that day to conduct the auction. He told the story this way:

It happens that the one man in all the world who was interested in a used race boat was in the room when I spoke. He stood up — a slim, dark-haired man in his mid-30s whom I had never seen before. "How much do you want for that boat?" he called out from the back of the dining room. Silence swept the room. The man did not look like he could buy the boat. I leaned over to the chairman and asked, "Shall I tell him the price?" "Sure," said [chairman] Judge Callender, "take a chance." I straightened up and told the stranger $1,800. The dark-haired man stood up again and said, "I've got $1,000 with me and I'll sign a six month's note for the balance." I leaned over to the judge and whispered, "Is his note good?" The judge smiled and said, "His word is good for a million," and *Miss Detroit* was sold to Gar Wood.

Overtaken by excitement and curiosity, Wood sped north to the small town on the St. Clair River where he could see his race boat and revel in the delight of owning *Miss Detroit*. He realized as he neared Algonac that he had just made a giant leap toward his boyhood vision of becoming a great race boat champion. The dream started to materialize, and he could feel the rush within himself as time for fulfillment was getting close at hand.

As soon as Gar Wood arrived at Algonac he located the C. C. Smith Boat and Engine Company on Pointe du Chene. He spotted *Miss Detroit* in a large open shed. His examination confirmed that her hull was as bad as reported. Jay Smith, Chris's oldest son, went over to talk to Wood. Soon Chris joined them in the shed, and the three men shared opinions and ideas on racing and boat construction.

Wood's mechanical knowledge and attention to detail helped establish a comfortable rapport with the Smiths. Wood introduced himself and let them know that just a few hours earlier he became the new owner of *Miss Detroit*. This was especially good news to the Smiths, because it meant that the final payment on *Miss Detroit* was finally ensured.

Boatbuilder Chris Smith was not a person to be discouraged easily. He had been through tough times before. This time it was different because his sons and now their families were also dependent on the prosperity of the boat business. Two of their best race boat customers, Baldy Ryan and Stuart Blackton, had fallen on hard times and would never again be in a position to have a Smith-built custom race boat. With America involved in World War I, there were few customers interested in the expense of owning a racing

boat. It was a perilous time for the 54-year-old boat-builder and his sons. Their combined talent was responsible for designing and building *Miss Detroit*, and now, a full year after its completion and a Gold Cup victory, they had not been paid in full. The craft was no longer in condition to successfully race again. It was at times like this that Chris Smith wished he had followed his vision of building pleasure boats for a larger market to encourage affordable family boating rather than racing.

It did not take long before Smith and Wood realized that they could gain a great deal by working together. Wood needed an experienced race boat builder to help achieve his racing goals. Smith needed a customer of means who could provide work for the family boatworks. The idea seemed to be advantageous for both parties. They agreed upon a plan that day in which Wood became the majority owner of the C. C. Smith Boat and Engine Company and the Smiths became his race boat builders. Gar Wood and Chris Smith were about to become boat-building partners.

When Wood returned to Detroit that evening, he was the owner of a broken-down race boat and a financially troubled boatyard. It was still a great day for the

At the 1918 Gold Cup Regatta the Wood brothers formed an unbeatable team. Arranged by age for this rare photograph, from left: Harvey, 43; Garfield, 38; Winfield, 36; Logan, 34; George, 32; Edward, 30; Philip, 28; Lewis, 26; and Clinton, 24. *Mystic Seaport, Rosenfeld Collection, Mystic, Connecticut*

two new partners and each had reason to celebrate in his own way. It was the dawn of a new era in boat-building and establishing new speed records. For the next six years Chris Smith and his sons created world-class speedboats under Gar Wood's personal direction, and the sport of racing on water changed forever.

The new partners immediately set plans in motion to replace the battered *Miss Detroit* with a newly designed hull in order to win the 1917 Gold Cup. Using the same 250-horsepower Sterling engine that powered *Miss Detroit* to victory in 1915, they designed a stronger and lighter hull that could stand up to the punishment of rough water at high speed. Jay Smith and Wood spent a lot of time together preparing *Miss Detroit II* for the Gold Cup. Jay would be Gar's onboard mechanic, and they made a strong and unbeatable team winning every event in 1917, including Gar Wood's first Gold Cup championship.

Up until *Miss Detroit* won the Gold Cup in 1915, the event had been dominated by eastern racers. After losing in 1916 to *Miss Minneapolis* and now to *Miss Detroit II*, the eastern racing associations were becoming increasingly irritated by the growing strength of the midwestern racers who had just taken their third straight Gold Cup. The old guard eastern racers were determined to make a serious effort to return the trophy and the race course to the East, where they felt it belonged.

Wood became aware of the mood among the eastern racers and knew that a major effort was now under way to regain the Gold Cup. He realized that he was going to have to step up to a new level of performance if he planned to retain the cup. He concentrated his efforts on converting a Glen Curtiss aircraft engine to a marine application. At the same time he told Jay and Bernard Smith to begin working on a new hull that would ride entirely out of the water from the bow to the step. She would be powered by a lightweight aircraft engine that would turn its propeller over 2,000 revolutions per minute. She would be *Miss Detroit III* and would open a great new era for race boats with aircraft engines. Gar Wood was about to make another breakthrough in his quest for speed.

The team of Gar Wood and Jay Smith won the 1918 Gold Cup with their aero-marine engine in *Miss Detroit III* and continued winning through 1921. Then the rules committee of the American Power Boat Association decided to step in and exert its will over Wood's domination of their race. In an obvious attempt to end Wood's mastery of the event, the rules committee outlawed the use of aircraft engines in the Gold Cup races.

Never before had the rules governing a major sporting event been purposely changed to lessen the dominance of its own champion. The change created a heated controversy within the entire race boat community. The rules committee stood its ground and disallowed hydroplane-type hulls entirely in favor of "safer" displacement hulls and limited engines to 625 cubic inches of piston displacement.

The rules change accomplished something that no one else had been able to do. It halted Gar Wood's string of Gold Cup victories at five. The rules committee had so diminished the prestige of the Gold Cup, that it was no longer interesting to Wood. He simply devoted his attention to international unlimited hydroplane competition. In 1920 he won the coveted International Harmsworth Trophy in England in spectacular fashion, establishing himself as an American hero in the eyes of the press. This event between nations was the epitome of world-class racing. It was in England at these races that the world was introduced to the first of the Miss America–type hydroplanes. Over the next 12 years racing enthusiasts were treated to nine more Miss Americas from the creative talents of Gar Wood and his team of race boat builders.

Chris Smith, on the other hand, saw the rules change in an entirely different light. He visualized this change in the rules as a great opportunity to promote recreational speedboats to an expanded market of sportsmen and boating families. He was convinced that the concept of the gentleman's runabout would open a vast new market for people who wanted to be part of the growing interest in boating. His hunch was that this may be the opportunity his family needed to finally make its mark in the boat business.

The arrangement with Gar Wood had been very advantageous to the Smiths and probably saved the family boat business at the most critical period in its development. Now enjoying a measure of security, the partnership was becoming less comfortable to Jay and Bernard who wanted to separate themselves from building the new racing craft that Wood was constantly envisioning. Chris Smith was 61, and time was getting short if they were going to go on their own once more. The Smiths knew it was now or never and made the decision to break their six-year partnership with Wood.

Wood's personal wealth and racing accomplishments were growing rapidly. He thought the Smiths were taking an unnecessary risk and was annoyed at their decision; however, he agreed to buy out the balance of the Smiths' interest in the boatyard on Pointe du Chene so that the Smiths could build a new factory on a large tract of open land in Algonac. The Smiths also agreed to continue to build stock 33-foot Baby Gar hulls for Gar Wood. Wood needed a supply of boats in which his men could install the Liberty marine engines that were being remanufactured by his recently created Detroit Marine-Aero Engine Company.

The deal was accomplished without a serious rift between the two former partners. There was even speculation that Wood was an investor in the Smiths' new operation to help them start up their new factory. They had shared more success in the past six years than many partners could expect in a lifetime. It was clear that they had different goals in their approach to boating, but their paths soon crossed and the two former partners became fierce crosstown, boatbuilding rivals.

Chris Smith and his sons had always wanted to develop a full line of affordable family boats. In their previous experiences with wealthy race boat enthusiasts as their prime customers, they often experienced lapses when their customer's racing interests were redirected to a new activity. More often, however, the money simply ran out for these flash-in-the-pan race boat customers.

Their relationship with Wood had been more successful than they ever imagined when they agreed to work together in 1916. As good as it had been, they wanted a more fulfilling role in boatbuilding. The Smith family was willing to put its modest life savings on the line, put in the long hours, and make the sacrifices necessary to try to reach its goal. The Smiths knew they had a good reputation for building fast, high-quality boats and believed there

Inside the Detroit Marine-Aero Engine Company, one of Gar Wood's many enterprises. For 20 years Gar Wood converted thousands of surplus World War I Liberty aircraft engines into the world's most famous marine powerplants. *Gar Wood*

were enough potential customers available for them to make a strong start. Together they had $8,000, and with this capital they made the decision to reestablish themselves as a totally independent boat-building family business called Chris Smith and Sons Boat Company.

A generous portion of early boat production by the new Chris Smith and Sons Boat Company came directly from their agreement to build Baby Gar hulls for Gar Wood's Liberty engines. Records show that the first 24 Baby Gar runabouts were actually built in the Smith factory and then shipped across town to Wood's Pointe du Chene facility. Here Gar Wood's mechanics installed the converted Liberty aircraft engines into the hulls prior to customer delivery.

As business increased for both enterprises their working relationship and the goodwill between them wore thin. Wood's generous contract for 33-foot hulls was diminishing in importance to the Smiths as their own business began to flourish. The contract with Wood was not as profitable to the Smiths as the direct sale of their boats to their own customers and their new dealer network. On top of this there were reports of quality-control problems and growing irritation that some of their best work was being directed toward the boats built for Gar Wood's racing competitors.

Then there was a major flare-up in the Fisher-Allison Race that would pit Chris Smith and Jesse Vincent of Packard Motors directly against Gar Wood in a controversy that would determine the winner of the race. Wood's boat, Teddy, driven by his brother George took the lead on the 34th lap of the race, passing Col. Jesse Vincent in the Packard Chriscraft II as its engine began to misfire. As Teddy moved into a comfortable lead its engine hatch cover blew off the boat. In order to qualify for prize money, the rules stated that the winning boat must finish with all the equipment intact. On the 45th lap, Teddy made a pit stop and retrieved the hatch cover. With the hatch back in place, Teddy finished the final five laps in first place. After the race tension was high, Chris Smith and his son Jay, who built Packard Chriscraft II, let everyone know that Vincent, who finished second, had a valid protest. The Smiths said Wood's boat should be disqualified. In the end, Vincent decided not to file a protest, but Wood's victory was diminished by the unnecessary controversy created by the Smiths.

From this moment forward the relationship between Wood and the Smiths fundamentally changed. Gar Wood decided to build his own boats and compete, head to head, with the Smiths by offering a more appealing and a more expensive boat as an alternative for the discriminating customer.

The two key boatbuilders on Wood's staff were Nap Lisee and George Joachim. He told them to expand the facilities and to seek the best boat carpenters in the area to build their own Baby Gar hulls. They enticed some of Smith's most experienced woodworkers and boat carpenters to join Wood by offering them higher wages. Lisee was responsible for designing and supervising the construction of all of Gar Wood's racing craft, custom boats, and all the famous Miss Americas. Joachim was the plant superintendent responsible for all operations connected with the standardized boat production. As his talent emerged, he became the person responsible for many new designs and the special styling that became the hallmark of Gar Wood Boats. For the next two decades this loyal and talented staff gained worldwide attention for developing the most attractive and best performing production boats in the world.

Gar Wood's well-publicized racing success resulted in a growing market for the powerful engines that were used in his various racing boats. Sensing another financial opportunity, Wood purchased as many government surplus Liberty aircraft engines as he could locate. He paid only pennies on the dollar for these superb engines that were still in their original crates and carefully prepared with preservative treatment. In all he was able to gather about 4,500 Liberties from various manufacturers and established a new operation called the Detroit-Marine-Aero Engine Company to convert these lightweight and powerful engines to marine use. They were installed in all the 33-foot Baby Gar runabouts in either the standard 400-horsepower model or the high-speed model at 500 horsepower. Gar Wood Liberty engines were sold to various boatbuilders whose customers wanted high-speed performance. Gar Wood cruisers, including Gar Sr. and Gar Jr. II models, had Liberty engines as standard power. By the mid-1920s Gar Wood Liberties were considered the hottest and most desirable performance engines in the boating industry.

Wood said that he sold 1,500 Liberty engines to the Soviet Union to help the country build training planes to establish its air force in the mid-1920s.

Wood's unparalleled reputation as a speed champion attracted many wealthy sportsmen who could not pass up the opportunity to impress their friends by owning a 33-foot Baby Gar runabout that was powered by a magnificent aircraft engine. In 1924 a typical Baby Gar runabout sold for nearly $12,000, which at the time was three times the cost of the average three-bedroom home in America. The prestige of owning a

Baby Gar was so special that the names of famous owners appeared in national boating magazine advertisements under the banner "Who Owns Baby Gars?" It was one of the most talked about ads ever to appear in a boating journal and more than likely the most-read boating ad of all time. When Gar Wood displayed the Baby Gar at the 1925 National Motor Boat Show in New York, it was the most heralded debut in show history. It was at this time that Wood's puzzling association with Howard Lyon developed. Lyon was an enterprising New York promoter who for a brief period was a major distributor of Gar Wood Boats before his breech with the Wood organization. He went on to start his own company, Sea-Lyon Boats.

With his brother Logan demonstrating astute leadership over the growing industrial complex, Wood virtually gave Logan total responsibility. By 1922 Wood was practically an absentee owner of the hydraulic hoist business. He spent far more time with his race boats than with the business that was financing his racing obsession. Wood's employees saw little of him unless they worked on his boats or spent their vacations at race time running errands for the race boat crews. His absence hardly seemed

In 1923 Gar Wood built this stunning 70-foot express cruiser for tobacco mogul Gordon Hammersley of New York. It was named *Cigarette* and powered with five Liberty engines. Later it was recognized as a prototype for the high-performance PT boat of World War II. *Gar Wood*

GAR WOOD . . . *America's Speed King*

Gar Wood, World's Champion Speed Boat Driver and head of Gar Wood Industries, knows motors as few men do. When he talks about horse-power he has a real message for you.

"Yes . . I use Fire-Chief gasoline!"

AND in that one simple statement Gar Wood sums up for you a speed expert's conclusions based on his own experience as well as laboratory analysis.

We might tell you the technical "whys" and "wherefores" of Texaco *Fire-Chief's* superiority. But we believe that *you* are much more interested in performance—not what *Fire-Chief* is but what it will do for you in the engine of your car.

In *Fire-Chief* you have a gasoline that will give you more for your money. Some motorists buy *Fire-Chief* because it's long on miles. Others like it because of its smooth action even on the toughest hill.

Gar Wood insists on this "emergency" gasoline because it produces winning speed and power from his engines.

Try a tankful in *your* car and you will understand why this gasoline is selected by men who know motors. You will agree with Gar Wood when he says "*Fire-Chief* is the finest gasoline I ever used."

THE TEXAS COMPANY · *Texaco Petroleum Products*

TEXACO *FIRE-CHIEF*
"EMERGENCY" ACTION IN EVERY DROP

Gar Wood was an international luminary and a popular national hero. He was sought by major manufacturers of his time to endorse their products, as so many modern celebrities do today.

Gar Wood's American Race Team in Cowes, England, ready to do battle for the coveted Harmsworth Trophy in 1920. From left: Bernard Smith, Clarence Mericle, Jay Smith, Gar Wood, and Phil Wood.

to harm the company. Wood was making money all the time and would eventually own four houses, a hunting lodge, and Cornelius Vanderbilt's Fisher Island Estate in Biscayne Bay. To get from place to place, he began to fly his own planes. He was a jet-setter before the term was coined. Flying became a new passion in his life, second only to his racing boats.

Wood's love for racing and flying did not, however, turn his eye away from watching the company's profits. Though he seemed to spend freely on his boat business and his homes, Wood was aware of where each dollar went. He interwove his individual and corporate entities so thoroughly that it was impossible to tell where the man ended and the company began. The hoist business put $377,000 into his Detroit house at Grayhaven. It paid for all the racing boats. Company

officers, who knew all too well of the boss's thrift in such matters as salaries, winced when the bills came in for $2,400 for new connecting rods for the racing engines. Of the $522,000 that Gar Wood Industries lost in 1932, $250,000 went into building and operating *Miss America X*.

Wood's heroic status resulting from his racing accomplishments had enormous value to his manufacturing company, Gar Wood Industries. His name was synonymous with winning, quality engineering, and precise attention to detail. All of these attributes were important to his customers. His name was so well recognized that he was asked to appear in product endorsements by giant corporations such as Packard Motors and Texaco Petroleum. These endorsements took place long before this type of product promotion became popular.

Gar Wood knew what he had in the hoist business—a small, profitable company. To keep it that way, his brother Logan ran the operation with unerring skill. He bought up competitors swiftly and expanded operations carefully. By 1933 the company got into the heating business because Gar Wood wanted an efficient furnace for his home. When he could not find one that he liked, he designed his own, and it worked so well he went into the business. Soon their new furnace designs were among the best and most efficient in the industry, claiming a remarkable 85 percent efficiency rating. Logan paid $25,000 to obtain new winch patents and then expanded into building tank bodies for trucks. These two decisions would prove invaluable to Gar Wood Industries during World War II by accounting for nearly half their sales on defense contracts.

In 1934 Wood took a brief excursion into bus manufacturing using the innovative and revolutionary designs of noted industrial designer William Stout. After building 175 Gar Wood buses, they realized that they were inadvertently competing with some of their best hoist and body customers. They sold the bus division and replaced it with bulldozers and earth-moving equipment. By the start of World War II, Gar Wood was the nation's largest producer of truck bodies, winches, cranes, and tractor attachments. All of these products were vital to America's national defense and resulted in substantial government contracts. A major advantage to Gar Wood's wartime volume was that the company was able to fill its government contracts with normal production since its products could be used readily in military applications as manufactured.

Until 1936 Gar Wood Industries was virtually a one-owner company. Of the 800,000 shares of common stock, Wood owned 780,000 shares himself. Later that year he sold 320,000 shares to a large Detroit syndicate because his brother Logan was in poor health and Wood thought it wise to make his personal holdings more liquid. In 1938 Logan, who had directed Gar Wood Industries so astutely, died. This was a grave loss to Gar Wood, because Logan had provided him with the freedom to pursue a successful racing career without the need to worry about the business's leadership in his absence.

Over the next three years Gar Wood sold the balance of his common stock and then in 1945, at age 65, he retired as chairman of the board. The new officers were all veteran company men, and one of the first moves of the new board was to overhaul management salaries that had lagged far behind similar positions in other industries. The second move was to hire the well-known design firm of Norman Bel Geddes to restyle the company's whole product line from boats to bulldozers, under the supposition that handsome bulldozers would sell better than ugly ones.

From its unplanned beginnings in 1922, the boatbuilding operation of Gar Wood Industries grew to become one of the major influences on pleasure boating throughout the world. Yet the boat division never accounted for more than 3 percent of the total annual sales of Gar Wood Industries. This modest sales figure provides a stark realization of the vast size of the industry that was required to finance Gar Wood's racing endeavors. This data also reveals the source of support for the boat division in the post-Depression years when boat sales slowed to a crawl. Wood used this enormous financial support system to ensure that quality would not be compromised with low-priced boats to stimulate sales. Gar Wood was not ready to allow his reputation for quality to be tarnished by the sudden setback to the national economy. His passion for quality, even during the hardest of hard times, is another example of the consistency of Gar Wood's values and his uncompromising character.

Gar Wood's Yen for Competition

Sportsman, Adversary, Champion, Boatbuilder

For Gar Wood, racing began to take a firm hold in 1914 when he went to Peoria with *Little Leading Lady* and won every race he could enter. He loved winning, and it was especially sweet in a boat that he designed and built himself. He knew that his growing hoist business still needed his full attention to develop its maximum potential. Only then could it sustain high goals for serious racing in the years ahead.

To the dismay of the mighty New York Central Railroad, scores of reporters and photographers were waiting at the Columbia Yacht Club when Gar Wood beat the crack *Twentieth Century Limited* from Albany to New York City by 21 minutes.

23

One of Wood's passions was cruising in remote areas of the Great Lakes. In 1916 he cruised to Georgian Bay, and on his return trip he entered his express cruiser in a special feature race as part of Detroit's first Gold Cup Regatta. He won the race but withdrew his boat when a protest was made that his cruiser did not comply with the express cruiser rating system. His sportsmanship in this matter was so much appreciated by a number of Detroiters that he was presented with a special cup.

Late in 1916 Wood felt that the time was right to launch his racing plans in earnest. He planned to attend a special luncheon in downtown Detroit where he heard that *Miss Detroit* was going to be auctioned to the highest bidder. This boat, a racing hydroplane, was the defending Gold Cup champion. It turned out that he was the only bidder and became the new owner of a boat with a seriously strained hull. Wood had done his homework, however, and knew that

Miss Detroit's powerful Sterling engine was in excellent condition and very competitive. It was this engine that was really the object of his bidding. Using the Sterling engine from *Miss Detroit*, Wood had his new boatbuilding partner, Chris Smith, build a stronger, faster *Miss Detroit II* and won the 1917 Gold Cup with the engine from the 1915 champion. It was a smart move and the beginning of 18 years of racing supremacy.

The following year Wood and Smith built *Miss Detroit III,* which would be the first hydroplane to be successfully equipped with an aircraft engine, a Curtis Model 12. With this special boat he won the Thousand Islands Trophy and the 1918 Gold Cup once again. He also finished first in the Canadian International Gold Challenge Trophy Race at Toronto but was disqualified after the race for cutting a stake.

Wood still had *Miss Detroit II* and with this boat captured the Webb Trophy in the Mississippi Valley

In 1914 Gar Wood won every race he entered with *Little Leading Lady,* a boat he designed and built himself. *Mystic Seaport, Rosenfeld Collection, Mystic, Connecticut*

A new 50-foot Gar Jr. II Flyer hull being water-tested on the St. Clair River near the Algonac plant in 1921. These custom-built express cruisers were tested for speed and performance before the cabin structures were installed.

Regatta at Moline, Illinois. In 1919 Wood again brought out *Miss Detroit III* to defend his Gold Cup Trophy, and this splendid craft gave its owner his third consecutive championship.

It was after this race that Wood began laying definite plans for an overseas race. England at the time held the coveted Harmsworth Trophy, emblematic of the World's Speedboat Championship. England had held the trophy for several years and fully expected to retain it. Wood had every intention to successfully bring it back to the United States.

Gar Wood, Chris Smith, and their extraordinary craftsman and designer Nap Lisee made plans to build two new race boats to make their challenge successful. Both would be twin-engined hydroplanes but slightly different in design and purpose. One would be *Miss Detroit V* and the other would be *Miss America*, the first of the world's most famous series of race boats to carry this name.

When asked by writer William S. Dutton if he believed in luck, Gar Wood replied, "In life's experiences there may be a chain of circumstances that seem to cause the fickle Goddess of Fortune to smile upon someone, but as for luck, I believe in most instances it follows preparedness and the person who leaves anything to luck is taking a long chance."

Preparedness, not luck, was one of Gar Wood's keys to success, and that is why he took two race boats to England to bring the Harmsworth Trophy back to America. *Miss America* was designed to perform well in smooth seas, and the heavier and longer *Miss Detroit V* was better suited for rough water conditions. Both boats, however, were capable of winning the race in any circumstance if one or the other broke down or was disabled. The British had expected that the American challenger would bring a heavy-seas boat with him, and Gar wasn't a bit surprised when the defender, who had the privilege, chose to race on a day when the sea was mill-pond flat. The "Silver Fox" of Algonac, as Wood was known, simply unwrapped the first of his great Miss Americas.

It was a costly undertaking to ship two race boats and two crews to England for the 1920 British International Trophy Race. The expense was of little matter to Wood because his goal was clear—capturing the Harmsworth Trophy for America. The race was held at Cowes, Isle of Wight, on August 10 and 11. *Miss America*, averaging 66 miles per hour, won the event with *Miss Detroit V* finishing second.

Wood returned home with the Harmsworth Trophy in supreme triumph and became one of America's most celebrated champions. In September he won his fifth consecutive Gold Cup. He also won the One-Mile North American Championship, racing *Miss America* at 78.2 miles per hour, faster than any motorboat had ever traveled. The record mile also showed how much reserve speed *Miss America* was capable of using if necessary in the Harmsworth race.

Clearly the American press had a new and colorful hero who was just beginning his assault on water speed records. The reporters loved this modest, articulate, self-made millionaire who never disappointed the news media.

In the fall of 1920 he shipped his sleek, new 50-foot express cruiser, *Gar Jr. II*, to Miami, Florida, for the Express Cruiser Championships and won. He entered and won two more ocean races while in Florida. Then in the spring he staged one of his famous media events. He decided to drive his express cruiser from Miami to New York City in less time than the famous express train *The Havana Special*. The media loved it. Wood made sure the press was given all the details of his challenge so that photographers could cover the event in detail. At the helm of the *Gar Jr. II* Wood covered the 1,260-mile trip in 47 hours and 23 minutes in all kinds of weather conditions, including heavy fog that forced him to go 25 miles offshore. He still beat the crack train by 21 minutes. He was so delighted with the media coverage

he decided to set an additional record by continuing on to Detroit via the Hudson River, through the New York State Barge Canal and Lake Erie, a distance of 2,200 miles in 84 hours. Using the news media to his advantage became second nature to Wood.

Wood's dominance of the boat-racing scene prompted his vanquished competitors to lobby racing authorities for rules changes to reduce his advantages. When V-drives were banned, Wood built *Baby Gar IV* as a 33-foot runabout with a standard direct drive. V-drive transmissions provided Wood with tremendous flexibility in selecting the optimum hull position for his powerful engines. By using a V-drive gearbox, the proper propeller shaft angle could be achieved wherever the engine was located. To power the *Baby Gar IV,* he designed and built a special short-stroke V-12 Liberty engine with 1,060 cubic-inch displacement, which was within the allowable tolerances.

Baby Gar IV made its racing debut in the popular Buffalo Launch Club Regatta on the Niagara River in 1924. It was at this event that Gar Wood and his mechanic, Orlin Johnson, dressed in formal attire, including top hats with chin straps, to demonstrate that their boat was, indeed, a "gentleman's runabout." They won all three heats of the Fisher-Allison Trophy Race, and the press loved the show. Wood's message to the rules committee was not lost

Gar Wood's personal 50-foot Gar Jr. II Flyer on a fast cruise. This versatile boat is equipped with a removable hardtop and removable windshield for racing. *Gar Wood*

With their life jackets secured, Bruin and Teddy in the lap of Gar Wood are ready to exceed 100 miles per hour in *Miss America IX* in 1931.

Teddy Bear Mascots

Early in Gar's career, Murlen Wood gave her husband a pair of small bears for good luck prior to a difficult race. He was happy to have them and secured them to the steering column of his boat. After winning the race, Gar said that having the two bears with him must have been the difference between winning and finishing second. He placed great value on the presence of the bears and named the bears Bruin and Teddy. He became convinced that he needed the bears with him to win. Only once did he forget the bears, and when he lost the race he believed that not having the bears was the reason he didn't win. He was convinced that their power was real and would never race again without them.

When *Miss America VI* disintegrated in its initial high-speed test with the mascots aboard, Wood thought the bears had saved him and Orlin Johnson from certain death. In the salvage operations, the divers were instructed to find the steering column because the bears were secured to it. They found the bears, and Murlen made two tiny life jackets for the mascots. The bears were very important to Gar Wood, who considered them a critical element in his success.

by the reporters, who sent photos of the well-dressed victors to all the wire services. It was another stunning media event for Wood, and pictures of him in formal dress created one of the most famous images in boat-racing history.

Perhaps the most widely covered race between a speedboat and a famous express train took place in the spring of 1925, when Wood raced the New York Central's crack *Twentieth Century Limited* from Albany to New York City in his gentleman's runabout, *Baby Gar IV*. Reporters from New York City newspapers said it was an event of great public interest in which the entire 138-mile course was lined with spectators, and the local Hudson River trains running at the time were filled to capacity. In spite of threats of punishment, school children in towns along the Hudson took the opportunity to view the unique event, and they no doubt felt rewarded for their truancy. A large crowd of spectators lined the banks and Riverside Drive to see the finish of the race at the Columbia Yacht Club.

Tens of thousands, perhaps even millions, who were unable to reach the river were kept in touch with the progress of the train and the boat by radio. Half a dozen airplanes accompanied the boats, one of them broadcasting a minute-by-minute account, which was rebroadcast through stations in New York City and Schenectady. This showdown between an express train and a racing boat so captivated the public that the New York dailies carried front-page accounts of the race for several days, before and after the race.

When Wood first announced his intention to race the *Twentieth Century Limited* from Albany to New York on May 26, 1925, the New York Central Railroad promptly announced that, as far as they were concerned, there would be no race. The train would maintain its regular schedule. Wood's persistence and the public's interest, however, soon overcame the railroad's reluctance. Forty years later, during a television interview, the train's conductor said it was his most exciting experience ever in all his years on the railroad.

Once again Gar Wood demonstrated his skill and his sense of preparedness. He began the race with two boats, *Baby Gar IV* and *Baby Gar V,* which were similar 33-foot "stock" runabouts. When the race began Wood was in *Baby Gar V* with his brother George in *Baby Gar IV*. Midway through the race, however, Gar switched boats while running due to engine roughness in *Baby Gar V*. He beat the train by 21 minutes in *IV*. It was a superb promotion and again demonstrated that Wood's good fortune and his resourcefulness were never far apart.

On one occasion, at a testimonial dinner in his honor, Wood acknowledged the five big strokes of

The all-new 1927 26-foot Baby Gar Jr. enjoyed a whirlwind success with more than 100 boats sold in its first year. By 1928 it was abruptly dropped from production with the departure of Howard Lyon. *Mystic Seaport, Rosenfeld Collection, Mystic, Connecticut*

luck in his life. He told the gathering, "My mother, my father, my 12 brothers and sisters, my first job, and my wife are the best breaks of fortune that I've ever had, or could have had."

Gar Wood was in many ways a modest man. He loved a challenge and worked hard at everything he did. He did not drink alcohol and only smoked an occasional cigarette. He was in bed by 10:30 P.M., and by 5:30 A.M. he was ready for a day's work. He ate intelligently rather than sparingly, enjoying fish, fresh vegetables, and fruit.

He was fond of well-tailored clothes but wore them carelessly. He loved piano and organ music but didn't play a single note. His Grayhaven home had one of the finest private organ installations in America. He would spend hundreds of thousands of dollars on what he believed to be value received and protest vigorously if overcharged on even a small item.

He called himself a fatalist and subscribed to the rule that a sport without risk was not worthwhile. Yet he was always careful that his planes and boats were in perfect condition at all times and never went in a boat without a life jacket. He was left-handed and played golf that way. He seldom read newspapers and only those articles called to his attention. He read with great interest autobiographies of prominent men in industry and men of accomplishment and devoured technical books on a wide range of subjects.

All of his brothers were solid achievers and quite successful. George and Edward were co-owners on the Locktite Patch Company in Detroit, one of the largest automobile tire patch firms in the world. Winfield was president of the Everlock Patch Company in Minneapolis. Logan managed Gar Wood Industries, Lewis was the chief engineer, Clinton managed production, Philip was in charge of the Canadian branch, and Harvey was responsible for overseas operations.

They were an extraordinary family where their parents brought them up to "be thankful to God that

Gar Wood and Jay Smith in their last photo together as teammates in 1921. Soon they would become boatbuilding competitors and fierce rivals for a related market. *Detroit News*

he's given you the strength to work." In the winter when the roads were closed and the children couldn't get to Sunday school, their mother took out the family Bible and held Sunday school in the parlor. Their big stove in the center of the room was stuffed with wood, and they all gathered about it as Mother Wood read to them from the Bible. Gar described these winter Sundays this way, according to William S. Dotton's "My First Big Stroke of Luck" that appeared in *The American Magazine:* "She'd tell us that she didn't want us to lie, or to cheat, or to smoke and drink and be shiftless. There're nine of us boys alive today (1922), and not one is a smoking or a drinking man. More than that, not one of us is ashamed of anything the others have done, and the credit belongs to Mother."

Gar Wood had a magnetic personality that seemed to engender deep-seated loyalty from his family and employees. He gathered teams of highly skilled craftsmen with a talent for solving the most vexing challenges. They stayed with him for years, many until they were too old or too infirm to work. Boatbuilders of the region were modestly paid in relation to the skills they brought to the job. Working for Gar Wood had the benefit of working for the man who was recognized as the best in the world in speedboat racing. He not only won, he beat other nations who used all their national resources to beat him. When Gar Wood won, all his employees and their families took part in the celebrations. He made sure that employees' families were given areas to view the races, and many were aboard large boats to watch from the best locations. Yet he was never generous in the wages and salaries paid to his staff. At the same time, he was always quick to put cash in the hands of anyone who did him a favor or performed a task in an exceptional manner.

In the small town of Algonac that was home to both Chris-Craft and Gar Wood's boat division, there is a noticeable warmth and enthusiasm when

The christening ceremony for *Miss America V* in 1926 was a media event in Algonac. On the deck of *Miss America* are Gar Wood, Orlin Johnson, Junior Wood, A. A. Schantz, and Murlen Wood. *Detroit News*

discussing Gar Wood's legacy to the area. The same is not true among the families that worked for Chris-Craft. They still express bitterness over the abandonment of their community when the giant boatbuilder moved its operations away from its roots and relocated to Florida. The Smith family was never particularly generous to its employees or to the community needs of Algonac. It was rumored that one of the last members of the Smith family in the community talked about her desire to relocate all the buried family members away from Algonac as an expression of her disdain for the criticism the relocation engendered.

Gar Wood loved cruising, exploring new waterways, and sport fishing, and he designed his boats to serve several purposes. All his cruisers were high-performance express models, and whenever he could, Wood entered them in races. In 1919 he had his boatbuilding partner, Chris Smith, build a 36-foot express cruiser called *Gar Jr.* and power it with a Liberty engine. It looked like a 36-foot runabout with a large sedan cabin far forward, followed by a decked-over engine compartment and an aft cockpit with a removable hardtop cabin enclosure. This interesting cruiser was capable of speeds in excess of 40 miles per hour and won races from Detroit to Miami over the next two seasons. Features of this hull design would show up a decade later on the popular 38-foot Chris-Craft Commuter.

After Wood sold *Gar Jr.* in Miami he worked out the details of a new 50-foot express cruiser design that he would power with two Liberty engines. It was called *Gar Jr. II.* Wood tested its performance before he installed the cabin enclosures, and those who saw it in this stage thought it was a giant runabout. After the cabins were installed Wood designed a clever windshield and hardtop that was removable for racing, giving this cruiser two distinctive profiles. In the

Motor Boating Magazine's Praise for Gar Wood

Charles Chapman, editor of Motor Boating magazine, became a close friend of Gar Wood and knew him well. They cruised extensively together. Chapman was in Baby Gar IV in 1925 when they beat the express train to New York City. He was so impressed with Gar's approach to boat design and operation that he wrote an almost unprecedented endorsement of Gar Wood Boats. The piece did not just praise a single model but the unerring care and dedication that Wood put into everything he did with boats.

Gar Wood has spent millions of dollars on his boats. Much of this should be charged up to development and experience but it has given him a vast fund of knowledge to draw upon which he has always put to good use in every boat he has designed and built.

Gar Wood is peculiar in one way. He has his own ideas. He embodies these ideas into his boats. He never steals ideas from others. If his ideas are new and untried or, perhaps, of doubtful value, he tries them out himself. He finds out. He builds dozens of boats to experiment with and then junks them in the development process. Few men could afford this, even if they had the desire or inclination. Boats are Gar Wood's hobby. He does not do it for financial gain— simply for the fun and to learn something which he can afterward put into practice for someone else to profit by.

The whole history of Gar Wood's connection with boats has been just this. His races have been more than mere sporting events, they have been the laboratory from which many scientific facts and practical solutions have resulted, not for his personal benefit alone but for the whole sport and the industry of boating. Every person that owns a modern motor craft today has profited.

Aside from Commodore Wood's racing craft, his other boats are well known. His Gar Jr. Cruisers and his Baby Gar runabouts are known and talked about wherever the wind blows and boats float. Now comes his new 26 footer which he calls the Baby Gar Jr. It will be more than a mere manufactured product. It is the tangible result of his long boating experience.

Some who do not know Gar Wood as well as I do, perhaps, picture him as a reckless, careless speed maniac. But this is just what he is not. While it may be true that he has lost count of the number of speedboats he has owned and although I have sailed with many racing and cruising skippers, under many conditions of storm and sea, still I have yet to find one as cautious, serious minded and conscientious as Gar Wood when he is at the helm. His whole thoughts are of safety and of others. All his boats have been the acme of perfection. He accepts nothing as ready until he knows by experiments, developments and experience that it is ready.

The various technical details and specifications of the new Baby Gar Jr. do not matter. The fact that the craft is a Gar Wood product is sufficient guarantee of its quality. No one needs to have any more concern as to the thickness of its planking or whether the frames are of the proper strength or material or correctly spaced than he would in

An original pen-and-ink portrait by artist Charles E. Pont in 1921 commemorates the major international victory for the Harmsworth Trophy in England by Gar Wood in *Miss America*.

the tensile strength of the steel used in the chassis of a Marmon car. The fact that a six-cylinder Scripps Marine Engine is standard, is but a further guarantee.

Gar Wood is a man of detail as well as one of organization. He watches the design and construction of all of his boats down to the most minute part. Yet he has built around him, as well, a group of men that know boats and engines and have grown up with them. — Charles Chapman, editor, *Motor Boating*

These statements constitute a remarkable endorsement from one of the most respected names in the field of motorboat publications. Most editors of major boating journals were always conservative and careful not to offend their other advertisers. Yet Chapman knew that Wood's reputation for quality and detail was becoming so widely accepted that his observations would not be seriously challenged. What was important was that, in 1927, Chapman was making it clear that Gar Wood's standardized production boats were about to set higher standards of quality and performance for the boating industry.

speed trials prior to the special express cruiser races at the 1920 Gold Cup, *Gar Jr. II* averaged better than 47 miles per hour. This is the boat that would beat the *Havana Special* from Miami to New York the following spring. It garnered so much publicity that Wood offered it as a stock boat—the Gar Jr. Flyer—and at least six were built.

Gordon Hamersley, a New York tobacco mogul, was well known as one of the foremost enthusiasts of fast express cruisers. His 55-footer, *Cigarette*, was thought by many to be the fastest boat of her size in America. At the express cruiser races in Florida, however, Wood defeated *Cigarette* in *Gar Jr. II*. As a result Hamersley entrusted Wood with building him a super express cruiser that would be capable of 50 miles per hour to transport him in comfort from his home on Long Island to his office in downtown Manhattan.

The idea was a great challenge for Wood, and he was delighted to take the assignment and create something special. The result was a beautiful 70-foot hull that was powered by five 12-cylinder Wood-Liberty marine engines of 450 horsepower each for a total of 2,250 horsepower driving triple screws. The port and starboard screws were driven by two engines each. The center screw was turned by a single engine used for maneuvering, getting under way, making landings, and for operating at slow speeds. On this one engine alone the boat could make 8 to 10 miles per hour at 1,200 to 1,500 rpm.

The 70-foot *Cigarette* was one of the first craft built by Gar Wood after Chris Smith and his sons broke their partnership with Wood in 1922. It was a big undertaking for Wood and his new team of boat carpenters in the small Algonac plant. Yet they were absolutely up to the task, and *Cigarette* has survived the many decades since its completion in 1923. The boat was delivered to Hamersley after an 800-mile maiden trip in which she operated superbly and was covered by marine writer Walter Bailey for *Motor Boating* magazine.

In an unusual turn of events, Hamersley returned the boat to Wood two years later to purchase a 50-foot Gar Jr. Flyer at the request of Mrs.

Gar Wood's first express cruiser, the 36-foot Liberty-powered *Gar Jr.*, being filmed in 1919 from an airplane during a special cruiser race. The craft was offered as a $14,000 stock model by C. C. Smith Boat and Engine Company in its sales catalog.

Hamersley, who had become fearful of the larger boat. The Flyer was powered with twin Liberty engines and also named *Cigarette*.

Wood requested permission to change the name of the 70-foot *Cigarette* to *Gar Sr*. He kept the big express cruiser for several years and repowered it frequently doing extensive testing related to military applications. Wood felt strongly that high-speed military boats the size of *Gar Sr*. could bring torpedo warfare into shipping lanes that large slow ships could not. With this unusual boat Wood was instrumental in suggesting the early PT boat designs for the U.S. Department of the Navy.

In 1942 a *Chicago Tribune* editorial stated, "Among the great inventors of modern weapons, this nation should not forget Gar Wood. He did more than any other American to develop the speedboat. He developed it as a racing craft, not merely as a record smasher in time trials. Necessarily, the boats he built and drove had to have maneuverability along with their speed. Mr. Wood can be justly acclaimed as the inventor of the PT Boat, as John Phillip Holland is for the submarine, the Wrights are for the airplane, and Ericcson is of the turret-armed battleship. Others contributed, as they did to each of the other weapons named, but in every instance there is one mind that coordinates and makes the stride forward which stamps the device as practicable; and, in the case of the PT Boats, it was Wood and his racing craft."

Harry Le Duc of the *Detroit News* reported Wood's role in the development of PT boats in his October 27, 1942, column this way: "Gar Wood was the first man to put an airplane motor in a boat and make it run, and the PT Boats today are powered with airplane motors that were re-engineered by the holder of the Harmsworth Trophy.

"Wood was the first man to design a hull strong enough to handle multiple installations of airplane motors and make world-record speeds with a creation that remained maneuverable. And it doesn't take an expert eye today to see the PT's, though longer and beamier, are related in design."

In 1930 Wood demonstrated the maneuverability and speed of his craft to Franklin Delano Roosevelt, a former assistant secretary of the Navy. Roosevelt was impressed, but the Navy brass was less than enthusiastic over these relatively small craft and far more interested at the time in allocations for large vessels. Yet the time of the PT Boats would soon arrive, and their value to the successful victory at sea would be firmly established in American naval history.

It was a golden time for Gar Wood. His small boat factory in Algonac was turning out high-quality boats that were a reflection of his standards of excellence, and demand for his boats was as great as their facilities would permit. Gar Wood Boats were clearly the most prestigious in boating for those who could afford them. The demand for these boats was growing rapidly, and it became apparent that the limited facilities in the Algonac boat factory would not accommodate increased production. Boatbuilding was still a hobby to Wood. His hydraulic hoist business was growing at a phenomenal rate and provided all the income necessary for him to achieve everything he wished. The boats that carried his name would never compromise quality or performance because there was no pressure to make a profit. To be sure, Wood was not planning to lose money while building high-quality boats, nor did he let his boat plant workers feel the plant could operate in the red. He insisted on designs and quality levels that would not be compromised, and each member of his staff understood his intent.

Wood maintained a residence in Algonac and spent more time at the boat factory than most people realized. He was able to do this because his brother Logan was a superb administrator and ran Gar Wood Industries with all the adroitness needed of a top industrial executive. In addition, all the other family members involved in the hoist industry provided loyal and valuable leadership that permitted Gar to devote time to racing and the fledgling boat business.

It is accurate to say that Gar Wood was personally involved in every design of the stock boats that carried his name. Wood often included personal messages in the sales brochures that clearly stated his involvement in the design and styling of every Gar Wood model. In one brochure his message in part was, "It is my desire to make plain that Gar Wood, Incorporated, is not merely the custodian and user of my name, but is, instead, a definite expression of my personal desire in the field of motorboating. For my part, I reserve the final approval of every new design and the right to insist that it shall conform in every particular with those principles of construction that I have personally developed and established."

The message was clear. Experimental designs that didn't meet his performance standards were never offered for sale. Wood's personal involvement is the reason that every Gar Wood Boat is an outstanding performer and why they are the choice of collectors. There has never been a poor-performing Gar Wood offered to the boating public.

The "Baby Gar"

The Ultimate Gentleman's Runabout, 1922 to 1929

By the end of the 1921 racing season, Gar Wood had won his fifth straight Gold Cup championship, and it appeared there were few challengers with the resources to contest his domination of this prestigious North American race. The Gold Cup rules committee was under pressure to do something creative with the eligibility rules to provide challengers with a better opportunity to beat Gar

This 1928 model Baby has a 500 horsepower Gar Wood Liberty aircraft engine. This boat was originally displayed at the 1928 New York Boat Show and sold to famous sportsman Caleb Bragg. It is now part of the Gar Wood Collection at the Antique Boat Museum in Clayton, New York. *Classic Boating*

Wood. The eastern racers were frustrated that they had been unable to bring home the Gold Cup to their prestigious yacht clubs and hold the race in the East where they felt it belonged. Some racers felt the unlimited qualifications of the racing rules made any serious challenge to Wood's powerful race boats just too expensive and too dangerous.

During the winter months the rules committee met to resolve this issue. In early spring the committee announced its plans for changes to the 1922 Gold Cup Regatta. The new rules placed restrictions on engines and hulls to encourage participation by boats that could be used for recreational boating when not involved in racing. It was a stunning turn of events that was clearly aimed at thwarting Gar Wood's domination of the Gold Cup Races. Those in the Wood camp felt the committee had caved-in to pressure from the East. These unprecedented changes would accomplish their purpose but also remove much of the glamour and excitement from the Gold Cup Regatta.

The new rules limited engine displacement to 625 cubic inches, essentially eliminating aircraft-type engines. Boats had to be a minimum of 25 feet of waterline length, have four-passenger capacity, wet exhaust, and an enclosed engine with hatches, and the hull had to be a displacement type rather than the hydroplane style (no steps). The intent was to develop boats of dual purpose that could race and be used for recreation as well.

For some time Wood had been refining the design of his 33-foot runabouts for long-distance racing and other open water events for which this type of hull was well suited. The 33-foot Baby Gar hull was a superb design that was as rugged as it was beautiful. Even though the decision of the rules committee annoyed Wood, he was still confident that he could win under the new rules with his Baby Gar.

Wood underestimated the effectiveness of the new rules in limiting his dominance. Built as they were for engines of tremendous power, Wood's boats were greatly impeded by the engine displacement limit. His frustration emerged quickly as less skilled drivers were able to keep pace with his docile craft under the new rules. When he lost to Jesse Vincent, who was driving a Chris Smith–built version of one of his own Baby Gar hulls in the 1922 Gold Cup, Wood was furious.

In 1923 he decided to build a new boat, *Curtis Baby Gar,* which he believed had the capability to win. He fell just short in this attempt as well, and in 1924 with *Baby America,* a radical new design, he made another attempt to recapture the Gold Cup. *Baby America,* a 25-foot direct drive runabout was powered by a modified "half" Liberty engine for Gold Cup racing and then re-powered by a Liberty V-12 for the Sweepstakes races. In 1925, Wood introduced *Baby America II,* a beautiful 26-foot all mahogany finished Gold Cup challenger. The boat ran well but

The breathtaking design elements and blazing speed of the Baby Gar runabout made this boat the first choice of wealthy sportsmen. *Helen A,* originally built for William Wrigley of Chicago in 1926, is now a Lake Tahoe favorite. *Roy Dryer*

once again Wood failed to win the Gold Cup. By 1929 the Gold Cup rules were modified to all step hulls once more, but Wood's full attention was focused on breaking the 100-mile per hour barrier and successfully defending the Harmsworth Trophy. He never challenged for the Gold Cup again. It was his last bid at this event. Wood loved unlimited races where he could fully involve his engineering genius along with his helmsmanship. Under the limitations of the new rules, the race lost its attractiveness.

One of the ironies from the politically motivated rules changes was the development of the "gentleman's runabout." But the most significant consequence of the rules changes may have been that they provided Chris Smith and his sons with the extra motivation necessary to separate themselves from Gar Wood. Under the new rules the Smiths had built faster boats for Wood's competitors in Wood's own shop. While this upset Wood, it also helped to expose the important differences between the Smiths' and Woods' vision of the future of boating in America.

Jay Smith, Chris's oldest son, persuaded his father that it was the proper time to make the break with Wood. He had been Gar Wood's riding mechanic and chief engineer for six years. Jay was convinced that racing would always be Wood's first priority and building affordable pleasure boats may never be important to him. Sixty-two-year-old Chris Smith was less anxious to risk everything on another new business venture. He had been there before; however, Jay was ambitious and eager and had the full support of his brothers, Bernard, Owen, and Hamilton. They prevailed on their father and together the Smiths made the decision that resulted in Chris-Craft, the world's largest manufacturer of motorboats.

Wood was surprised at the Smiths' decision but was not deeply troubled by it. He bought the Smiths' share of the partnership, including the old Smith boatworks property on Pointe du Chene in Algonac. This provided the Smiths with the additional capital necessary to finance their enterprise. Wood planned to build his own race craft under the direction of Nap Lisee, who still enjoyed designing fast boats for Wood. In a gesture that would help both enterprises, Wood contracted with the Smiths to build Baby Gar hulls for him. This gave the Smiths a jump start in their new venture and provided Wood with a good source for his 33-foot hulls. A ready supply of these hulls was vital for Wood's new Liberty marine engine business.

The Liberty aircraft engine of World War I was designed and guided into production by Jesse Vincent of the Packard Motor Car Company and J. G. Hall of

Even the aft cockpit of the Baby Gar runabout provided luxurious leather seating with room to spare. Passengers loved the sensation of riding so far aft at high speed in this big boat.

the Hall-Scott Motor Company. It was the first aircraft engine mass produced with standardized components in the United States. In February 1916 Packard produced a 12-cylinder engine with cylinders set in blocks of three and in banks of six at an inclined angle of 60 degrees. This engine was the basis for a new design approved by the Army and Navy Production Board. They named the new engine the "Liberty" because the first test model was inspected on Independence Day 1917, only 33 days after the first drawings of it were started. The British government promptly ordered 1,000 of them upon completion of the endurance tests. Before the Armistice came, Packard was producing as many as 900 of the engines per month.

Before surplus Liberty engines were available from the government, component parts and unfinished engines were available in the Detroit area where most of the engines were manufactured. Howard Grant, an enterprising government inspector, saw the potential here and purchased unfinished engines and assembled them as Grant Motors. It was a Jay Smith–converted Grant-Liberty that powered the Gar Jr. in, perhaps, the first successful marine conversion of a Liberty airplane engine. Wood liked the performance of the Liberty engine and repowered *Miss Detroit II* and *Miss Detroit III* with Grant Liberty engines. In 1921 Wood purchased a railcar load of Liberty engines directly from the government. This substantial inventory

Gar Wood's exclusive Manhattan showroom attracted many wealthy New York buyers. This was the way to select a speedboat in the pre-Depression era. *Mystic Seaport, Rosenfeld Collection, Mystic, Connecticut*

allowed him to establish the Detroit Marine-Aero Engine Company.

With Jay Smith and Carl Fisher they designed the components necessary to successfully convert the Liberty airplane engines to reliable marine use, and a new Wood enterprise was about to begin.

For some time there had been growing interest in runabouts as recreational craft, as well as an interest in modified racing. Many of Wood's wealthy friends were looking for fast, safe boats that could provide competitive excitement without the danger of extreme speed. With his abundance of Liberty engines, Wood saw a new opportunity he couldn't resist. To him it made perfect sense to design a craft that would suit the developing interest in runabouts and provide a suitable boat for his marine engine conversions. Together with Carl Fisher they established class rules that would permit the use of his Liberty conversions in displacement hulls with a

minimum length of 32 feet, wet exhaust, marine transmissions, optional V-drive, and seating for at least four. With these characteristics in mind Wood and Smith designed the first "Baby Gar" runabout. It proved to be a successful design and won the Wood-Fisher trophy regattas in Detroit in 1921 and in Miami in 1922. Later *Baby Gar II* retired the trophy when it won in the 1922 Detroit Regatta. Later that year *Baby Gar II* won the Sweepstakes sanctioned Detroit Regatta for the third time. According to the rules, a racer that had won the trophy three times would permanently retire the trophy and be allowed to keep it.

Gar Wood researcher, Craig Magnusson, traced this period for his 1997 *Rudder* magazine article. "Not satisfied with winning his own series with the original Baby Gar, Wood commissioned Smith to build a Fisher-Allison Trophy version to be raced at the Fisher-Allison contest scheduled for Hamilton,

Ontario, during August 1922. Gar Wood knew his large Liberty would not be allowed, but convinced himself that twin DMA 300 horsepower Fiats should qualify as standard marine engines, insofar as his company had over 500 in stock and was selling the marine conversions as regular marine engines. However, the narrow hulled Baby Gar design (6-feet 6-inches) did not lend itself to twin shafts, so he created an amazingly complex transmission to combine both engines into a single powerplant driving a single shaft. The two straight 6, 1,326-cubic-inch engines sat side by side in the engine compartment, angled together at the front where they both drove into the single gearbox V-drive unit. When both engines engaged, they connected solidly together and drove the single propeller with over 600 horsepower. This propulsion package was heavy, weighing over 3,000 pounds for both engines and gearbox, and required a taller than

Nap Lisee's watchful eye supervises every element of construction for the superb 33-foot Baby Gar in the Algonac shop during the mid-1920s. Note the early use of portable handheld power tools. *Morris Rosenfeld*

normal raised hatch to cover the tall engines. She was fast, though, capable of nearly 60 miles per hour.

"Gar Wood won the 1922 Hamilton Fisher Allison Regatta, was protested for using aircraft engines, and later disqualified."

In April 1922 the Chris Smith and Sons Boat Company purchased a full page ad in *Motor Boat* magazine to announce the formation of the new company. The company's ad listed four standard models being offered: a 24-foot for $2,200, a 26-foot for $3,000, a 26-foot rear drive for $2,800, and a 33-foot Baby Gar Type for $7,500.

Wood was surprised that his old partner was advertising a model called the "Baby Gar Type." The special name and the design were based on Gar Wood's specifications and had to be considered Wood's property. After some haggling between the two principals, Smith agreed to build Baby Gar hulls exclusively for Wood, and other similar craft would not be identified as Baby Gar Types (at least not in magazine ads).

Midway through 1929 Gar Wood discontinued the 33-foot Baby Gar with raised deck coamings and introduced this modern flush deck–style 33-foot runabout as its replacement in their line. *Morris Rosenfeld*

It was about this time that Howard Lyon, a New York City hotel proprietor, became increasingly interested in promoting and selling Gar Wood Boats. Lyon was a dapper, well-connected New Yorker with exceptional promotional skills. He offered to set up a permanent Gar Wood showroom in downtown Manhattan. It would be located in the prominent Hotel Barclay at Lexington and 49th Streets. Though he was intrigued by the idea and impressed by Lyon's style, Wood thought he might not be ready for a New York showroom just yet. Lyon was persistent, however, and by 1925 they agreed upon an arrangement in which Lyon would maintain a permanent Gar Wood showroom in New York. Lyon was a highly skillful pitchman, making impressive sales to prominent people. He ran spectacular double-page ads in boating magazines that featured his name in larger type than Gar Wood's logo. The official Gar Wood sales ledger shows that in a period of 13 months, Howard Lyon sold 14 33-foot Baby Gars and 41 26-foot Baby Gar Jrs. These sales amounted to 40 percent of Gar Wood's total production for the period.

Despite the apparent success of their cooperative effort, Lyon's sales tactics soon led to conflict.

Lyon was aggressive and took liberties in advertising and promotion that made Wood uneasy. He became critical of some construction methods and some of the standard details. He made delivery promises to his customers that were impossible for the boatbuilders to meet. He disagreed with Wood about dropping the popular 26-foot Baby Gar Jr. in favor of the new 28-foot Baby Gar runabout that had tested well and would be more profitable. The working relationship between the two strong personalities quickly began to fall apart. When Wood learned that Lyon was talking about introducing his own line of boats if their differences could not be resolved, he abruptly ended the relationship.

By the opening of the 1928 New York boat show Lyon was announcing his plans for the "Sea-Lyon" brand of runabouts that would be built at his boatyard in City Island, New York. He would offer five models: 24-foot, 28-foot, 30-foot, and 36-foot runabouts, and a 42-foot Purdy-designed Commuter. The 36-foot Sea-Lyon would be powered by a "Lyon-Tuttle" Liberty engine and claimed 60 miles per hour. Lyon was confident that he could successfully go head-to-head with Gar Wood in this highly specialized market. It was an ambitious plan

Two 1929 28-footers running side by side in this interesting factory photo. In the foreground is the raised-deck version and the far one is the redesigned flush deck style that replaced it.

considering Gar Wood offered only two models, the 28-foot and 33-foot Baby Gars, for 1928; and Chris-Craft offered just four hull sizes of runabouts.

Howard Lyon's sales literature reflected his enormous ego and his desire to upstage his rival boat manufacturers, and in particular Gar Wood, by pointing out the flaws of other established boatbuilders versus the benefits of his methods. A sample from his brochures advertises "deck planks only 2" wide, not 9" boards with grooves every 2" to simulate seams. . . mahogany costing two and half times the price of ordinary boat mahogany . . . upholstery of genuine cowhide, not second split or imitation leather, . . . springs covered with rubberized fabric instead of burlap. . . ." He made a point of stating that Sea-Lyon boats are tested on the rough seas of Long Island Sound rather than protected rivers or lakes where other boat manufacturers test their boats. Lyon refers to his competitors as "*distant* boat builders, that don't always understand the needs of (eastern) customers."

This original display ad introduced the new 28-foot Baby Gar 30 runabout to the boating world and a wider audience because it was more affordable and less complex than previous models. The V-bottom boat was powered by a Chrysler Imperial marine engine and attained a top speed of 30 miles per hour.

There are no production volume figures available on Sea-Lyon Boats. Fewer than a dozen Sea-Lyons are listed in the ACBS directory, which is a valid indicator of their modest production. The importance of good (or lucky) timing is a major factor in the ultimate success of boatbuilding enterprises. Sea-Lyon Boats never survived the post-Depression years and by 1932 ceased operations.

From 1922 to 1929 the boat that exemplified the epitome of pleasure speedboating was the 33-foot Baby Gar with its V-drive Liberty engine. There were 62 of these original Baby Gars delivered to some of the world's most noteworthy sportsmen. The Gar Wood sales ledger lists purchasers of Baby Gars with well-known names of John Dodge, William Randolph Hearst, Benjamin Guinness, Lord Louis Mountbatten, Norman Woolworth, Robert Ringling, Philip Wrigley,

and many others. Due to Howard Lyon's brazen, full-page ads that listed all of these prominent owners, it became common knowledge "who owns Baby Gars." This impressive list was intended to motivate other prominent people to join them and buy a Baby Gar, the latest symbol of success.

Owner motivation for this type of craft has not been lost in recent years. The desire to have a big, loud, fast boat costing two or three times the price of the average home is still in evidence on nearly every lake and river in America. Today they are called muscle boats, cigarettes, and off-shore racers.

The Baby Gar was described this way: "Not one distinctive feature, but the tout ensemble of design, finish, appearance, comfort and speed, causes every lover of water sports who has experienced the thrill of idling along at three miles an hour—and,

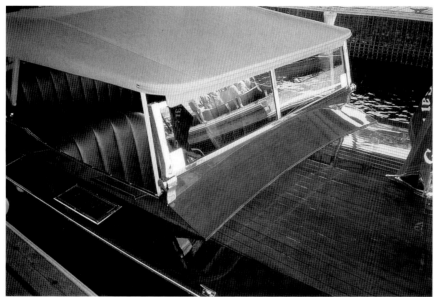

The "one-man" convertible top was a popular and practical option for Gar Wood runabouts. Its attractive design made it the most widely purchased factory option.

presto!—traveling faster than a limited train, to pronounce the Baby Gar the "aristocrat of motorboats."

The Baby Gar was taken directly from the prototype designs of Wood's trophy-winning boats of the same name. This was the race boat that beat the *Twentieth Century Limited* express train, fitted out with all the luxury features that passionate owners wished to have aboard their craft. There was no greater speedboat then, or now, for those who wanted what would be the finest of its breed.

The Chris-Craft archives confirm that the original Baby Gars built by Chris Smith had a beam of 6 feet, 4 inches. The beam was increased to 6 feet, 6 inches, and in 1925, when Wood's men began building their own hulls, the beam increased to 6 feet, 10 inches. By 1929 the beam was finally increased to 7 feet, 2 inches. Construction and materials were, as always, of the finest standards.

A special 18-page booklet prepared by Gar Wood carefully described every detail of the Baby Gar runabout.

The keel and chine are of carefully selected, strong fibrous mahogany, combining lightness with strength. The frame and ribs are of white oak. The keelson and engine timbers are of spruce. Weight has been eliminated wherever possible by the use of Canadian white pine. The bottom is planed first with a thin layer of diagonal mahogany planking. A layer of canvas, coated with white lead, is then applied on which is laid the outer, longitudinal planking of mahogany.

The sides are single planked mahogany, carefully selected and matched for color. The frames are made in sections to utilize the best grain of the wood. While this is expensive, it is the only type of construction strong enough for a fifty mile per hour boat.

The joints are carefully made and reinforced by a large butt block fastened with bronze carriage bolts. The keelsons extend the full length of the hull and are securely fastened to the transom, which is very rigidly framed. Spruce timber is used to reinforce the boat over the rudder, propeller and rear strut. This timber also holds the eighty gallon copper gas tank. A heavy brass plate is bolted to the hull over the propeller to protect the bottom at this point.

The forward cockpit is protected by a clear vision windshield of nonshatterable glass. The wide flare and the fact that the boat rides well out of the water make the windshield unnecessary for protection against water, but it is provided as a wind break and to protect the driver in stormy weather. The combination post and bow light, as well as all the other trimmings, are nickeled.

The forward cockpit is divided into two seats. The forward seat for the driver is within easy reach of all switches and instruments. The instruments are grouped on a single panel under glass and are lighted at night by a soft, indirect light. Convenient pockets are located at the side for small tools and gloves.

The rear seat is spacious and very handsomely appointed. A smoking kit and vanity case are within easy reach. The floor of varnished mahogany is protected by a neat perforated rubber mat.

The cushions are deep and comfortable. The Spanish leather upholstery of French Blue gives a rich contrast to the soft oil-rubbed mahogany. Rubber step-pads protect the varnish at all the cockpits.

The powerful twelve-cylinder Gar Wood Marine engine is located directly aft of the forward cockpit. The engine compartment is made accessible by two large hatches. This gives the engineer ready access to the large storage batteries and the water-cooled oil tank.

The engine is located well back, giving perfect balance to the boat. The forward drive, using a step-up gear box, gives but a small angle to the propeller shaft, allowing the boat to ride very flat on the water. This makes a very smooth riding boat in all kinds of weather.

On May 2, 1929, the final raised-deck 33-foot Baby Gar was shipped to William Greenow of Chicago. It was a limousine model, one of only three ever made. This was the 72nd Baby Gar in this great series of boats, including the five racing prototypes.

In 1927 Gar Wood had introduced a totally new boat that they would call the Baby Gar Jr. It was a striking 26-foot runabout with speed options to 40 miles per hour and offered at one-third the price of the 33-foot Baby Gar. There was also an elegant sedan model of the 26-foot Baby Gar Jr. that would account for nearly 25 percent of the year's sales.

The 26-foot hull was planked in choice African mahogany, upholstered in French blue Spanish leather, had all monel metal fittings and was finished with eight coats of clear lacquer. This was the first mention of the use of lacquer by Gar Wood. The brochure stated that "Lacquer is a radical improvement in boat finish, unaffected by sun, ice, gasoline, salt water or exposure to ordinary heat or cold. More durable than any varnish." The use of lacquer was a surprising, but short-lived, alternative to varnish.

In 1927 alone Wood built and sold 103 Baby Gar Jr. run-abouts and sedans. It was a remarkable sales record for the new company. The com-pany also introduced another model in midyear, a 28-foot runabout called the Baby Gar 28. The company built only seven of the 28s that year, but it was a supe-rior boat to the popular 26-foot Baby Gar Jr. A cost analysis showed that the 28 could be built for slightly more cost than the 26-footer and would command a much higher selling price. In a move that must have surprised observers, Wood decided to drop its best-selling boat for 1927 in favor of the 28-foot Baby Gar. It proved to be a good choice, and in 1928 the com-pany sold 70 units of the 28-foot Baby Gars. The pro-duction included 29 runabout models, 40 sedans, and 1 limousine. In addition it built and sold 8 of the larg-er 33-foot Baby Gars. All of this was accomplished without Howard Lyon who had accounted for 40 per-cent of its sales volume the previous year.

Production History for the 33-foot Runabout Hulls

Group I

1921 to 1924	**Baby Gar Gold Cup Boats**, I to V	total units: 5

Group II

1922 to 1925	**Smith-built Baby Gars**, No. 1–22	total units: 22
1925	**Baby Gars**, No. 23, 24	total units: 2
1926	**Baby Gars**, No. 25– 40	total units: 16
1927	**Baby Gars**, No. 41– 56	total units: 16
1928	**Baby Gars**, No. 57–No. 63	total units: 7
1929	**Baby Gars**, No. 64 –67	total units: 4

Group III

1929	**Flush-deck runabouts**, No. F3 –F10	total units: 8
1930	**Flush-deck runabouts**, No. 102–109	total units: 8
1934	**Flush-deck runabout**, No. 5460	total units: 1

Group IV

1941	**"Specials,"** No. 6630–No. 6643 (Target Boats)	total units: 8

Summary:

67	Classic raised-deck Baby Gars, three of which were limousines.
17	Flush-deck runabouts, one of which was a limousine.
8	"Specials," which were wider and had different features than the stock 33-foot runabouts. All the Specials were sold to the Intercontinent Corporation as government-specified Target Boats.

Production History for the 26-foot Baby Gar Jr.

	Baby Gar Jr.	total units:
1927	No. 2701 to No. 27103	103

Summary:
78 open runabouts: $3,500 to $4,000;
25 sedans

On June 1, 1929, the first 33-foot flush deck model runabout, the successor to the classic Baby Gar, was loaded on a railcar and shipped to John Wanamaker in New York City. It was a model "55" with a 500-horsepower Gar Wood Liberty engine. In 1929 the boat factory decided to begin to identify each model in a more specif-ic way by using the rate speed as the model code. The four model designations for 1929 were "30," "40," "50," and "55."

This system of model identification was used until 1935 when the variety of models was simply too numerous for this method to work effectively. If the runabouts were offered as an enclosed sedan or limousine model, then that specific designation would be added after the model number. Sedan and

Gar Wood attracted sportsmen who often requested special custom-built models. This 28-foot single-step hydroplane was built for Carlos de Beistequi and shipped to Paris for racing. *Morris Rosenfeld*

limousine enclosures were very popular and added from $600 to $2,000 to the open runabout price.

The 28-foot runabout series turned out to be an excellent model for Gar Wood. It was able to maintain the prestige of the 33-foot Baby Gar in a more practical size. With smaller, less complex engines the 28-footer was able to reach acceptable speeds. Most important was that the 28-foot model brought the quality and performance of the larger Baby Gar in a more affordable boat to a larger customer base. This model was nicely adaptable to enclosed versions with sedan, limousine, or landau tops, as well as the optional Kercheval folding convertible top.

It had become evident by the end of the decade that Gar Wood Boats were among the most sought-after by serious buyers. They lived up to the promise of quality implied by their name in every way. Wood insisted that boats bearing his name must be of the highest quality so as not to diminish his reputation. From 1922 to 1929 the Gar Wood Boat Company was responsible for building nearly 500 standardized runabouts, express cruisers, and special custom designs. In addition to accomplishing all this production for individual customers and dealers, Wood's new company built six Miss Americas: the *III, IV, V, VI, VII,* and *VIII,* as well as new Baby Gar's *IV, V, VI, VII,* and *VIII,* and the radically new

Baby Americas. It was a remarkable production achievement for someone who never intended to be in the boat business.

During this period, Wood established the new boatbuilding operation and designed new race craft. He also won the 1926 Fisher-Allison Trophy, defended the Harmsworth Trophy in 1926 and 1928, and set a world's speed record for the measured mile of 92.8 miles per hour in *Miss America VII.* He also beat the fastest scheduled express trains.

These accomplishments were of such magnitude that it's hard to compare them to anything else of their time. And while these activities were going on, Wood continued to encourage Logan to expand his industrial complex with uncompromising precision since this was his true source of income for racing.

Wood's boatbuilding success in Algonac exceeded that facility's ability to meet demand. Dealers and customers had to wait for their boats because sales exceeded production. Again, Wood was forced, by his own success, into directions that he had not planned to go. Expansion of the boat factory was essential to meet the boating public's growing desire to own a Gar Wood Boat. Available space for expansion did not exist at the Algonac site, which meant that an alternate location needed to be selected immediately to avoid further delivery delays.

1929 Model Designations by Maximum Speed

Stock Model	Description	Maximum Speed
Model 30	28-foot Runabout with Chrysler Majestic engine	30 miles per hour
Model 40	28-foot Runabout with Scripps 202, or Kermath	40 miles per hour
Model 50	33-foot Runabout with Gar Wood Liberty 400 horsepower	50 miles per hour
Model 55	33-foot Runabout with Gar Wood Liberty 500 horsepower	55 miles per hour

Production Volume for 1929

Stock model	Quantity	Price
Model 30 open	105	$2,950
Model 30 sedan	6	$3,550
Model 40 open	61	$4,500
Model 40 sedan	20	$5,100
Model 40 limousine	13	$5,350
Total 28-foot models	205	
Model 50 open	6	$8,950
Model 50 limousine	3	$10,950
Model 55 open	3	10,950
Total 33-foot models	12	

Special Custom Models

No. 2901	35-foot Special for Robert Oakman, Detroit	
No. 29 -1	36-foot Special limousine for John Shibe, Philadelphia	
No. 1	28-foot Hydro for Carlos de Beistequi, Paris, France	
No. 2	36-foot Hydro for W. S. Corby, Washington, D.C.	

The 33-foot flush deck runabout was a striking modernization of the original Baby Gar. Introduced in 1929 it represented the ultimate in standardized runabout design. Its potential production was severely reduced by the Depression. *Classic Boating*

Marysville, Michigan

Home of the World's Finest Boat Factory

The "world's finest boat factory" completed and ready to produce the world's best boats. The special highway bridge was constructed to provide river access for testing new boats. *Mystic Seaport, Rosenfeld Collection, Mystic, Connecticut*

It was a remarkable accomplishment that so many superb boats were produced in Gar Wood's limited facilities in Algonac. The impressive list of fabulous boats constructed in these modest shops includes world-class race boats, unlimited hydroplanes, gentleman's runabouts, limousines, and powerful express cruisers. Virtually every square foot of available space was pushed to the limit to make room for more production. By

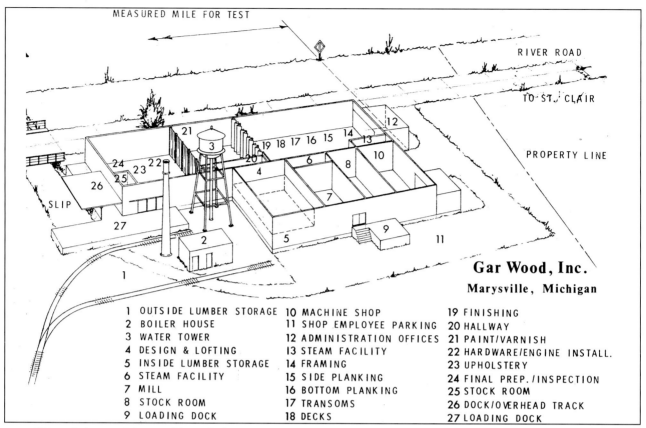

This scale layout of the new Marysville factory shows each department and operational function. The plant was a superb facility and for years claimed to be the world's most efficient boat factory. *Bill Lester*

1927 it was clear that there simply wasn't enough space to keep up with orders for new boats. Even Gar Wood, who never spent money unnecessarily, realized expansion was imperative.

Wood's men had enlarged the shops several times as production requirements made it necessary. Now there was no space left for another addition. The business that began for a limited number of boats was growing faster than Wood ever anticipated. He had assembled a superb crew of boatbuilders; with a larger more efficient boat factory they could double their volume immediately.

Wood decided that the facility in Algonac would continue to be used for building his race boats. It was well suited for special work, and it made sense to keep this work separate from their standardized production boats. It was also a good facility for building custom boats and express cruisers for special customers. Nap Lisee, chief architect and engineer for all Wood's race boats, was comfortable at Pointe Du Chene and would continue to be in charge of operations there.

Wood wanted George Joachim to be plant superintendent of the new factory because he understood production, had a strong sense for quality control, and was highly respected by the workers. Joachim had a superb eye for styling and had innovative design ideas. Wood was impressed with Joachim's suggestions and considered him a key to successfully expanding their line of standardized production boats. It was also a wise move to separate his two key men, Joachim and Lisee, so each could expand his special talents without encroaching on the other. Lisee would continue to design and build the fastest race boats in the world, and Joachim would develop the Gar Wood standardized boats into the world's most advanced production speedboats. Wood's first challenge was to select a suitable location for the new factory. It was essential to keep the site close to the Pointe Du Chene facilities, so that the two operations could share these facilities when necessary. It was also important for employees to travel easily to work in either factory. It was desirable for the new site to be on the river for testing finished boats and prototypes designs. The site consideration required a dedicated railroad spur to provide for the arrival of lumber and new engines and accommodate outgoing shipments of finished boats. The lack of adequate railroad spurs had been an annoying problem at Pointe Du Chene for years. Chris Smith controlled the railroad access to the Port Huron and Detroit Railroad. Jay Smith always made sure his company's needs were given railroad priority, to the constant dismay of Gar Wood's workers.

Ten years earlier, C. Harold Wills, the outstanding automobile pioneer, had selected the hamlet of Marysville to build his new automobile factory. He wanted to create a perfect planned community in Marysville for the workers who would be building his revolutionary new Wills Sainte Claire motor cars. Wills and his partner, John Lee, were top management administrators for the Ford Motor Company. They decided to leave their secure positions to start their own car company to build the "car of the future." Wills and Lee purchased more than 4,200 acres of land that included all of the present city of Marysville to build their factory and to plan the ideal community around it.

On February 19, 1921, the first Wills Sainte Claire automobile, a V-8, rolled off the assembly line. Marysville had grown from only 200 residents in 1919 to a booming town of 3,000 people by 1922. The Wills Sainte Claire was a superb automobile and was truly ahead of its time. Soaring production costs outstripped profits, however, and the company was finally forced to close in 1927.

The closing of the Wills Sainte Claire factory— the main employer in town—was a devastating blow to Marysville. The community was anxious to attract new manufacturing jobs to fill the void. Marysville was a nice place to live with a ready supply of skilled workers anxious for work.

Wood was well aware of Marysville's desire to attract new industry, but its location was further up river than Wood preferred to be. Nevertheless, he was curious to see if the town Marysville would offer an attractive enticement to build his new boat factory in the community. There was some ideal property right on the St. Clair River that could suit his needs.

Wood thought it might be possible to get the town leaders to provide what he wanted, including a railroad spur, access to the river, low cost utilities, property tax relief, and a low-interest building loan if he played his hand carefully. Wood's nickname, the Silver Fox, was attributed to the resourcefulness he often displayed in winning difficult races. His cool, almost disinterested approach to relocating to Marysville only served to convince the Marysville community fathers that he might have better offers from other sites along the river.

On October 10, 1929, in a remarkable expression of enthusiasm, 50 area business and professional men raised $45,000 among themselves to bring the new factory of Gar Wood, Incorporated, to Marysville. The *Port Huron Times Herald* reported, "It took just 17 minutes to raise the money. No more enthusiastic meeting of citizens was ever held in the city and when the proposition was put squarely before them, their response was immediate and whole-hearted." Later in the evening the chamber of commerce's industrial committee voted to pay the cost of the construction of the boat canal, giving the factory direct access to the St. Clair River to water test each boat as it was prepared for delivery. It was further reported at the meeting that "Mr. C. H. Wills had been most liberal in his treatment of the proposition, giving outright to the company 250' of River frontage and selling the rest of their River frontage at $50 per foot, which is considerably less than the market price for this property."

Everything seemed to be falling into place nicely for Gar Wood. Every concession he hoped for had been given, plus additional enticements that he had not expected. United States Savings agreed to carry the $85,000 mortgage for 10 years at 6 percent. The Eastern Michigan Railroad agreed to build a long siding and spur directly to the new factory to facilitate rail deliveries and transportation of finished boats. The highway department also agreed to build a bridge on River Road over an access canal to the St. Clair River.

The factory's mill room (#7) where all full-size patterns were located and lumber was prepared for planking and framing. In the background is the area for inside lumber storage (#5). The lofting and design departments (#4) were located above the limber storage. *Gar Wood*

The Otto Randolph Company of Chicago, contractors selected to build the factory, were on-site immediately to stake out the building. The contract drawn between the industrial committee of the chamber of commerce and Gar Wood specified two factory buildings: "The larger one to be 550 [feet] long by 70 [feet] wide and the other to be 350 [feet] long by 70 [feet] wide. The site of the new factory will occupy about 6 acres with 650 [feet] on the river front. The larger of the two buildings must be ready for occupancy by January 1, 1930, so that boat production can begin at this time. The second building must be completed by February 1, 1930."

The industrial committee anticipated that Gar Wood would employ 200 workers immediately and that number would increase as production grew. The *Port Huron Times Herald* reported, "Gar Wood is the speed boat king of the world! His boats are known all over the earth and shipments are made to all parts of the globe." It was October 10, 1929, and a new level of optimism and anticipation filled the hearts of everyone in St. Clair County, unaware that before the end of the month an unimaginable worldwide financial collapse would change everything.

Although the original plans called for two factory buildings, the final result was, in reality, one factory with a shared wall down the middle. The larger unit was 550 feet by 70 feet and would be the location of the production line. Along this line boat assembly activities would begin and proceed through the full length of the building emerging at the far end. The smaller unit was 350 feet by 70 feet and would house the services, parts, and materials needed to supply the assembly line activities.

A noteworthy aspect of the new factory was that it was being built by a highly successful industrialist who understood boatbuilding procedures as well as the value of production efficiency. His success in

This 240-foot long section of the factory was the assembly department where bottom, side, and deck planking took place. Production moved from south end to the north end of the factory. *Gar Wood*

business and his success as a racing champion meant that Wood was expected to design a superb boat-building facility. Wood looked forward to the challenge, and the resulting new factory would become one of the promotional features in Gar Wood advertising. Even before it was completed, brochures made references to "a splendid new plant at Marysville, Michigan, the first modern fire-proof factory devoted solely to the production of stock runabouts and the last word in boat building efficiency. . . ."

Every Gar Wood catalog from the time that the factory was finished featured photographs of the factory under the caption, "The world's most efficient boat plant." In most catalogs special features of the factory were described this way: ". . . the plant is equipped with the latest, modern wood working machines and overhead monorail systems to move hulls carefully through each department. Hundreds of visitors come to the great Gar Wood Boat plant each year and every visitor is deeply impressed by what he sees, no matter how small or relatively unimportant."

The production line side of the factory was divided into three general activity areas: woodworking, assembly, and finishing. Adapting assembly line methods from the state-of-the art auto industry, a new hull would begin when the keel was set and pre-cut frames were set in place on a strong back jig at the south end of the plant. From there it would move to the side planking station. Hulls were moved smoothly from this station by an overhead monorail system. The next location was the bottom planking area, where the hull was turned over and transom assemblies were installed. The hulls were returned to the upright position and lowered into concrete wells in the factory floor to facilitate deck installation without the need for ramps or scaffolding. The hulls then moved to the finishing area, where they were prepared for stain and varnish. Hardware, upholstery, and engines were added in the final area of the production line.

The finishing section could be separated from the other dusty activities of the production line by large folding doors. These large doors that extended from the floor to the ceiling were at each end of the finishing section and fit snugly into the walls when fully opened. When hulls were ready for paint or varnish, these giant folding doors were closed to form a tight seal separating this section from the rest of the factory activities. Within the folding doors, a special ventilation system controlled the humidity and temperature, and filtered the air all at the same time, to create a perfect dust-free environment for varnishing

This is the factory interior from the north end of the assembly department looking toward the administrative offices and main entrance. Note the wells in the concrete floor where hulls could be lowered to facilitate deck installation. *Gar Wood*

and painting. Gar Wood Boats were famous for their superb finishes, which included decks hand rubbed with pumice on every model up to 1942. The ads boasted that the company had the most modern and best-equipped finishing room in the industry, in which the air in the finishing section was completely changed and filtered six times each hour. When these doors were opened the entire length of the 500-foot production line could be viewed from any point in the building.

Gar Wood's greatest gift may have been his ability to assemble a team of highly talented people into a dedicated organization. He was able to inspire them to take their skills to new levels of achievement and to foster unusual loyalty and intense devotion to their work. Wood and his riding mechanic were directly responsible for winning the races. Nonetheless, each victory was accomplished in a complex state-of-the-art racing craft that was the product of Wood's team of creative talent. His men anticipated and solved problems that staggered the imagination. Turbochargers, transmissions, propellers, fuel chemistry, hull configurations, and friction coefficients were just a few of the considerations addressed in every new race boat Wood created.

The man Wood depended on to design, build, and fine tune every one of his race boat was Joseph Napoleon Lisee. Lisee was a master builder, designer, pattern-maker, wood turner, and perfectionist. To everyone who knew him he was affectionately called

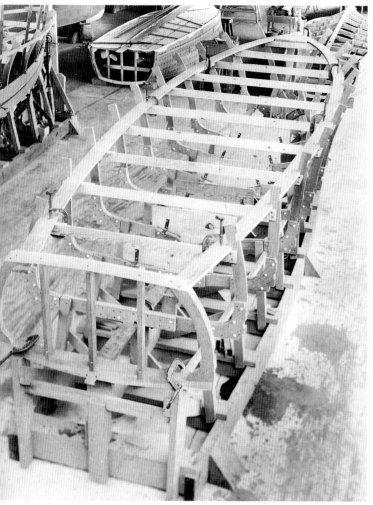

The first operation in hull construction began in the framing department with the setup rack. Here the precut keel, stem, and frames were placed in position in a special rack for a 22-foot runabout. *Gar Wood*

"Nap." He was a diminutive man of enormous talent who was hardly known out of his home community. He was modest to a fault, yet was the key person behind Gar Wood's reputation as the speedboat king of the world.

Lisee was born in Troy, New York, in 1871. His parents moved to Marine City, Michigan, when he was eight years old and by age twelve he began working at a local lumber mill. By the time he was sixteen he was considered one of the finest woodworkers in the entire region. In 1905 he pursued his interest in the boat-building industry by joining Chris Smith and Sons in Algonac. Smith quickly recognized Lisee's unusual talent for designing fast boats as well as his knowledge of the properties of marine lumber. It was Lisee's work that brought Baldy Ryan and Stuart Blackton to Smith to build the Reliance series of race boats. Lisee's *Miss Detroit* was the boat that successfully brought the Gold Cup to Detroit in 1915. Years later Gar Wood Jr. stated, "Although Chris Smith and his son Jay received credit for the designs of the Smith race boats, neither of them ever designed a single boat. The genius who designed, lofted and constructed all of Smith's racing boats was Nap Lisee."

Even with this success, the Smith boat company was in financial trouble and Lisee's future with the Smiths was uncertain. There were many weeks when payday at the Smith's boat shop had to be delayed and sometimes missed altogether. It was at this low point when Gar Wood entered the picture, purchased *Miss Detroit*, and subsequently became Smith's partner. Lisee was given the assignment to design and build *Miss Detroit II* for the new owner and would never miss a payday again. Lisee appreciated Wood's engineering knowledge and his recognition of quality woodwork. It was the beginning of an association and friendship that would last more than a quarter of a century. Over the next 16 years Nap Lisee designed and built more than 30 of the most famous race boats of all time. This included all the Miss Detroits, all the Baby Gars, all ten Miss Americas, the Baby Americas, and the Gar Jrs. Beyond this he was responsible for organizing the initial production of the standardized runabouts under the Gar Wood logo. He was also in charge of designing and building the 70-foot express cruiser, *Cigarette*, with five Liberty engines in 1923. All of the 50-foot Gar Jr. II express cruisers were his designs.

Lisee's incredible record of productivity for successful racing designs remains unmatched, yet few people recognize his name. He was a modest, unassuming man content with his valued association with Gar Wood. Wood admired his terse, tenacious style and his passion for perfection in his work. He could spot the slightest flaw in a hull and didn't pause for a moment to remedy it. Nap's son said one time, "I don't believe there was a finer woodworker in the country. He never used gauges or other measuring tools, he did his work by hand, his eye was sure and accurate. Why I believe he could spot an eighth-inch variance in a joint at 150 feet away. He knew wood and he knew boats. He constructed hulls from plans drawn full scale on the floor of the plant. He always was accurate and could be extremely fast when he had to."

One of Lisee's more publicized challenges took place in 1928. The recently completed *Miss America VI* was having its first high-speed test run on the St. Clair River in preparation for the Harmsworth Trophy Race. (This was thought to be the fastest Miss America so far.) Midway in the test run the boat was approaching 100 miles per hour when it virtually disintegrated. The exact cause was never determined, but the boat was a total loss. From his hospital room Wood told Lisee to "build another one." It was 17 days before the race and nearly everyone conceded that it was an impossible task. Lisee said that "if the divers can find the engines, I'll have a boat ready for them." In 17 days a totally new Miss America was ready and went on to successfully defend the trophy in the 1928 race with both Wood and Johnson at the controls.

When *Miss America IX* was given her first trial run, she galloped slightly. This characteristic was not one that either Wood or Lisee would tolerate in the boats. Their boats had to slide smoothly and evenly over the water. The boat made four runs up and down the river before Wood brought it back to the dock. There was no discussion; Lisee had observed the boat's performance. Wood threw him a glance of inquiry. Lisee nodded and said, "Haul her out." Lisee directed a slight, but critical alteration to the hull. The boat was launched immediately with Wood back at the controls. *Miss America IX* ran up the river without any perceptible gallop. Lisee smiled; the problem was solved.

Lisee claimed that his most unusual assignment was in 1923 when Wood asked him to design a 70-foot express cruiser for tobacco millionaire Gordon Hamersley. What made this boat so unusual is that Wood made special speed commitments to the owner guaranteeing speeds that could only be reached by installing five Liberty engines. It was a remarkable feat for Lisee, and it did what Wood promised, and that's all there was to it. The understanding between these men was so complete that spoken words were often superfluous.

Lisee may be best remembered for designing and building the final Miss America, number 10, in this fabulous series of race boats. With its four huge Packard engines it was almost beyond comprehension. Lisee was 60 years old when he completed this brute of a boat that set a long-standing world's record of 124-plus miles per hour.

One of Lisee's lesser known talents was the designing of several outboard racers for young Gar Wood Jr. These hulls were outstanding and provided Junior with 15 national class outboard championships and 42 national and international speed records. It was one of Lisee's hulls that was the first outboard to officially reach 90 miles per hour and unofficially reach 100 miles per hour in 1939.

By the late 1930s custom and specialized boat work at the Algonac shop had diminished. It appeared that Gar Wood's racing career was finished

and that there would be no challenges to the Harmsworth Trophy. Lisee designed boats for a Canadian boatbuilding firm called Mac-Craft across the river in Sarnia, but he was always available if Wood or Junior needed him for a special job.

During World War II Lisee was appointed superintendent of Mac-Craft Corporation of Ontario to supervise the building of the 112-foot Fairmile Class subchasers. In just six months, two of these large ships were launched into the St. Clair River, a full month ahead of schedule. He was particularly pleased in November 1941 that his wife of 45 years was afforded the honor of christening one of these ships officially identified as QO-63. Nap Lisee, one of the finest designers and builders of fast boats for 40 years, died in August 1946 at age 75.

One of the least recognized names among the principals of the Gar Wood story is George Joachim. Born in 1873 in St. Clair, Michigan, Joachim was the youngest of nine children born to German pioneers. Shipbuilding was a flourishing business in the region, and he began work in the shipyards as an apprentice. He also had a strong interest in music and studied formally with a teacher for several years. His musical training provided him with the necessary skills to teach others by offering piano and coronet lessons to local students.

In 1910 at age 37, Joachim was offered an unusual opportunity. Marine City, 8 miles south of St. Clair, was searching for someone to organize and direct its new city band. The town council heard about Joachim's fine reputation as a music instructor and offered him the position. To make the deal even more attractive, they also arranged to provide him a good position with the McLouth Shipyards along with housing in Marine City. It was an excellent opportunity, and he agreed to take the position and move his family to Marine City. At the McLouth Shipyard his job responsibilities were in molding, lofting, and design work. His design skills developed, and his knowledge of ship building grew rapidly. He enjoyed his working arrangements for several years. Then McLouth, which specialized in wood construction, experienced a gradual decline in production as steel construction became the norm for commercial ships.

Joachim had a growing interest in small craft and was attracted to the C. C. Smith Boat Company in Algonac. This small boatbuilder was making a name for itself building boats for Gar Wood, and he went to work for them shortly before they decided to split off on their own. His talent impressed Wood, and he asked Joachim to become part of his race boat building team along with Nap Lisee and other key people. Joachim had great respect for Lisee and knew he could learn a lot working closely with him. He also knew that Gar Wood had the wealth and persistence to provide him secure employment for the foreseeable future. He adapted Lisee's method of lofting new boats full size on the floor and went so far as to paint the floor of a spare room in his house jet black so he could lay out details full size at home.

In his spare time he began working on new design ideas to incorporate into the next production models. Unlike Lisee, Joachim enjoyed building scale models of his new designs so that he could better visualize their contours from all angles. He became involved in every phase of boat production and was well respected by all the workers. Because of his knowledge of each operation, he was able to suggest more efficient methods and techniques that improved production and reduced time on task. The men appreciated his ideas and listened carefully to his suggestions.

Joachim was able to make valuable contributions to the design of the express cruisers, custom boats, and the early standardized models. Lisee was the chief designer of the hull configuration, and Joachim added styling features. The two men worked well together and complemented each other's skill perfectly.

As the production of standardized models increased, Joachim's responsibilities expanded.

George Joachim and Napoleon Lisee at the lofting table in the design room No. 4. These men were the heart and soul of the Boat Division.

When a new race boat was being planned or built for Mr. Wood, Lisee would ask Joachim to supervise production and quality control for the building of the standardized boats.

When Wood decided to build the new factory at Marysville it was Lisee who suggested that Joachim should be the superintendent of the new operation. Ed Hancock concurred because it would allow Lisee to work exclusively on Wood's new race boats and the special custom boats. Whenever a new production boat was introduced, Lisee would get involved in laying out the hull design and testing the prototype. The new responsibilities and the working relationship seemed to be acceptable to the principal parties, and with this arrangement the new factory was opened.

By 1941 Gar Wood's standard boats were considered the pinnacle of design for their respective lengths and types. The Gar Wood hull featured a deep entry forward for a softer, drier ride. Pronounced flare forward, increased freeboard, and substantial beam ensured seaworthiness in rough seas. From this point on Gar Wood's styling took over and there was no mistaking the distinctive features that separated them from their rivals. The classic styling that draws people to Gar Wood Boats is the genius of George Joachim at its best. The pronounced crown of the decks, the formal stem line, the folding V-windshield, streamlined cabins, distinctive shear lines, and wide covering boards are all features created by Joachim. These are the features that Gar Wood enthusiasts find so attractive about their favorite boat and the features that give a particular manufacturer an advantage over another. George Joachim is one of the most important designers of the golden era and deserves to be more widely recognized for his enormous contributions.

Ed Hancock, general manager of the boat factory, joined the operation in 1923 and became one of the most respected men in the boatbuilding industry. Hancock was also the brother of Mrs. Edith Wood and received strong support from Logan in operating the boat plants in Algonac and Marysville. For 23 years he would be the key administrator for the boat division and was totally devoted to its success. He was responsible for much of the detail work in planning the new factory, all of Gar Wood's national boat show presentations, promotional advertising, press releases, and the fulfillment of the major defense contracts during World War II; the last of these duties led to Gar Wood earning the Army-Navy E Award for outstanding effort and production excellence.

Gar Wood's sales manager was the affable Jack Clifford. Clifford had been originally selected by the

Wills Sainte Claire Automobile Company to establish its nationwide dealer organization. He had been carefully picked by Wills for this plum position. In 1927, when the Wills Sainte Claire closed, Clifford was hired by the Chris Smith and Sons Boat Company to create a dealer network that would provide national distribution of the company's boats. He used the skills he learned setting up automobile dealerships for the Wills Company to establish the first international boat dealer organization for Chris-Craft. He was a stellar performer for the boat company, enlisting successful automobile dealers to expand their businesses to include boats. By 1931 he became a Depression casualty, as they were forced to let him go along with the talented Bill MacKerer. Hancock was well aware of Clifford's sales ability and talent for establishing good dealers. Hancock encouraged Logan Wood to support his recommendation to hire Clifford and establish their national and overseas dealership organization.

Ella Stewart was Jack Clifford's secretary for seven years from the time she joined the firm in 1935 until 1942. Miss Stewart was fresh out of the Detroit Business Institute in 1925 when she was hired by Chris Smith to assist his daughter, Catherine Smith, with the bookkeeping at Chris-Craft. Stewart had known Clifford from this period and recalled the forces that ended her employment there: "I worked at Chris-Craft from early 1925 until the summer of 1931, when the Depression suddenly descended with its drastic effect on all pleasure craft building, including Chris-Craft." Four years later she joined the staff at Gar Wood as Jack Clifford's secretary. The two former Chris-Craft employees made a great team. Miss Stewart could always be counted on to provide accurate information when Clifford was on the road visiting dealers or participating in boat shows. She knew all the dealers and they relied on her to do everything necessary to keep them informed about the progress on their orders.

Bill Lester, another key employee, had a special connection to secure his job at the Marysville plant. His grandfather lived in Marine City and was a neighbor of George Joachim, the plant superintendent. It was the spring of 1937 and the factory was busy. Bill was an excellent carpenter and draftsman, skills that were in demand. He was hired as an apprentice craftsman, and his first assignment was to select the correct shade of mahogany bung and insert them over the recessed brass screws. Even this basic task was examined carefully by the shop foreman to be sure the grain matched perfectly and that the bungs were trimmed flush. After demonstrating his skill at this job

The varnishing and painting room was sealed off from all other factory operations by an ingenious assembly of full-height folding doors. This arrangement provided complete regulation of air temperature, humidity levels, and air-filtering control. *Gar Wood*

he was promoted to inserting the corner blocks in the cabin roof of sedans and cruisers and shaped them with hand tools to the exact contours required. In time, as once again he demonstrated his ability to carry out this task to perfection, he moved up to completing the entire roof. Job assignments were highly specialized so that the employees given a particular task became quite expert at doing it. Under the watchful eye of George Joachim, nothing less than precise delivery of each job was the rule at Gar Wood.

In time Lester moved up to the drafting and lofting department, which was his first love and the assignment he always wanted. He made drawings of metal parts and boat deck plans used in brochures and promotional flyers. New boats were lofted full scale on a giant lofting table where patterns were created full size. Nap Lisee and Joachim worked together on new designs with Lisee concentrating on the bottom design and Joachim responsible for the overall styling of the new boat. Draftsmen like Lester would develop the patterns for framing the new hulls.

By the end of the 1937 season, Lester was laid off with many other workers; however, most of Gar Wood's employees in the 1930s were semiretired craftsmen or farmers with sustaining livelihoods, and this pattern of seasonal layoffs was anticipated and a way of life among the employees. Lester moved west and became a highly successful designer in the growing aircraft industry in California. Had he been able to stay with Gar Wood, he commented that he was sure he would have pursued a career as a naval architect in time.

Gar Wood's Marysville, Michigan, facility opened on New Year's Day 1930 as the world's newest and finest boat factory. It was a symbol of hope to a community that needed a boost to its depressed economy and everyone hoped that Gar Wood, the world's speedboat king, might just be the answer they needed. The factory was a superb facility, and production of 28-foot runabouts and 22-foot runabouts began on schedule. A full crew of carpenters, woodworkers, upholsterers, machinists, finishers, and office staff opened for business, and within a few weeks photographers were hired to capture the images on film. Each department was shown in full operation with boats in every stage of construction from a set of frames on a jig to a gleaming hull being lowered onto a rail car. Gar Wood's new factory was the envy of their competition.

One photograph in particular stood out above the others. It was taken from the extreme north end of the factory looking down the full length of the production line. In the foreground are hulls nearly completed followed by row after row of hulls in lesser stages of construction. There were 72 Gar Wood Boats in various stages of construction observable in this remarkable photograph of the entire production line. No one knew or could even imagine when this photo was snapped that it would be 16 years before this many boats would be on the production line again. It had been only four months since the stock market crash and the total effect was yet to be felt across the nation.

Working in the old, crowded Pointe du Chene yard in Algonac, Gar Wood's men produced 224 boats of the 28- and 33-foot types in 1929. They fully expected to double or triple that volume in the new factory. When the new factory produced only 193 boats in 1930, it was a disturbing disappointment to everyone. No one seemed to grasp the potential magnitude of the economic situation. Most people were sure that it was only a temporary condition that would soon pass. It seemed inconceivable that the anticipated prosperity that the new factory promised

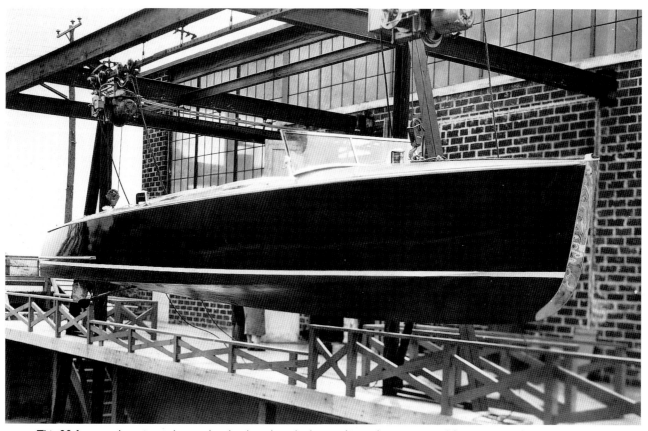

This 28-foot runabout is on the overhead rail ready to be lowered into the access canal for its required water test before shipment to its new owner. Every prewar Gar Wood was water tested before leaving the factory. *Gar Wood*

to so many families could vanish so soon. As disappointing as the 1930 production was at the time, they would not surpass it for six more years.

One by one, rival boatbuilders fell victim to the Depression and were forced to close. Fortunately Gar Wood's hoist business was strong and debt free. Although orders for new boats had slowed, Wood's industrial products continued to be in demand and his conservative approach to expansion placed him in a strong financial position. His pride in the boats that carried his name and his vast personal wealth would support the new factory and the boat business through this difficult period. The Marysville factory, designed to produce 600 custom quality boats annually, would never reach that volume. They would, however, proceed to build high-quality boats in spite of the economy. Their new models continued to represent the most attractive and advanced designs of their time. Quality was never compromised during these difficult years. In some ways the economic downturn motivated the creative genius of their staff to new heights, as they introduced splendid designs to lure new buyers.

The typical production period for the standardized Gar Wood Boats during the 1930s would be from February through August. In a very good year production might run through September. Employee layoffs usually began in early June, and by mid-July the staff was reduced to just key employees. Even seasonal employees were loyal to Gar Wood and understood the nature of the boat business. These men with extraordinary skills often had small farms or were lake sailors or had sideline trade activities to carry them through the year. They lived in a seasonal maritime region and understood that it was the way things were and they could get along.

The "off months" at the factory were occupied with work on new designs and building prototype boats. New designs and special boats were often prepared for the National Motor Boat Show in New York City in January and the Chicago show in March. Dealers' orders and direct sales at these two major boat shows made up the majority of Gar Wood's new production. The entire year's production was determined by the models ordered at the New York and Chicago boat shows. Sales brochures and price lists were always printed in preparation for these shows. All their major distributors were expected to attend and "work the show." Dealers were encouraged to place their orders at this time and were rewarded with various factory incentives. There were years where some models featured in the brochures were never produced due to insufficient interest at the national shows.

The new designs were built in November by a small number of key employees. These key employees usually supervised departments and possessed exceptional skills for which they were rewarded with year-round work. If work was slow at the boat factories, they would be assigned to Detroit to work Wood's other factories.

Logan Wood's son Bill liked to tell this story about how tough things were in 1933. During one particular stretch of time, his two uncles, Ed Hancock and Charlie Jones, were the only employees at the boat factory. They each worked 12 hours a day, seven days a week. Their most important function was to keep the coal-burning boiler fired up. Ed handled the office work and Charlie, who had the night shift, worked in the plant. Between them they filled orders for parts and actually completed two boats.

Gar Wood Industries and Gar Wood Inc., the boatbuilding company, were two separate operations. Gar Wood Inc. was Wood's personal boat business, which was an outgrowth of Wood's six-year partnership with Chris Smith. The boat business had always been financed by Wood with concealed contributions from Gar Wood Industries. In 1929 Gar Wood Inc., the boat company, signed three mortgage agreements for a total of $105,000 with the Marysville Improvement Company and United States Savings Bank on the new factory. The agreements required regular payments to reduce the debt completely over 10 years.

By 1935 little had actually been paid by Gar Wood Inc. toward the debt, and the creditors were becoming justifiably impatient. Walter Gaskins, treasurer of the Marysville Improvement Company, wrote the following: "In 1930, you paid the interest and the $2,000 on the principal, leaving a balance of $18,000. On November 13, 1931, you paid half a year's interest, and on February 10, 1932, you paid another half year's interest, making the interest paid up to December 7, 1931. The interest is now almost four years in arrears and the principal payments are five years in arrears. Conditions have been bad, we realize, but we feel that you should cooperate with us to some extent and make payments."

Wood took the public position that the boat business "should stand on its own feet." He had brought much needed employment to the area, the workers were always paid on schedule, and their products were recognized throughout the world. His factory was very specialized and there was no other industry ready to move in, so he felt confident that the mortgage holders could wait until the boat business improved.

When foreclosure was threatened, Ed Hancock, Gar Wood's general manager, responded, "We regret very much to advise that we are not in a position at this time to meet these payments. We are, however, in hopes that the boat business will improve to such an extent in another year that we can at least break even on our operations, and possibly show a small profit, at which time, we of course will want to meet our obligations. Each year since we have been in this plant we have operated at a tremendous loss." This letter was written at the end of the 1935 production year.

A year later, Gar Wood Inc. offered to settle the debt on all the mortgages for 20 cents on the dollar. This offer was rejected on the advice of C. Harold Wills, who now held a major position with the Chrysler Corporation and was still influential in the Marysville community. In 1937, however, the Silver Fox stepped in and settled each of the mortgages for a fraction of their original value. Having accomplished this, Gar Wood Industries promptly purchased the Marysville boat factory from Wood, and it officially became the Gar Wood Boat Division of Gar Wood Industries. Wood was likely handsomely paid for his boat factory.

As it turned out, 1937 was an outstanding year for Gar Wood with nearly 300 boats built and delivered. The company offered a wide range of handsome models and produced one of the most attractive sales catalogs with a full color cover. Just when it seemed that the future was bright for the boat division a curious internal decision made the employees understand what it meant to be a small part of a large industry.

Gar Wood Industries had expanded manufacturing cautiously into new product lines with success. One of their most interesting endeavors was their brief entry into the bus transportation business. Gar

For a brief time in the late 1930s Gar Wood Industries built buses. For more than a year these buses were completed in the boat factory in Marysville along with motor boats. The Gar Wood bus was a William Stout design and featured aircraft engineering. *Detroit Library*

Wood knew of William Stout when he was employed by Packard motors as chief engineer in the aircraft division working on the V-12 Liberty engine development. Stout left Packard shortly afterward and established himself as a creative designer with innovative ideas for motor transportation. He designed "sky cars" and "rail planes." His 1935 automobile, the rear-engine Stout Scarab, received wide acclaim and caught the attention of Detroit's top designers. Stout developed lightweight construction methods, which he applied to buses. Wood was impressed.

Most buses of the day used traditional bus construction involving a separately built body fitted onto a separately built chassis. Stout's design replaced the usual chassis with a framework of steel tubes that were welded together producing greater strength with a major reduction in weight. Lower weight meant increased gas mileage, which would be important to transportation operators looking for increased profits. The Stout 24-passenger bus weighed only 6,000 pounds. By using a rear-mounted Ford V-8 truck engine and the Ford suspension system, components were easily obtained and relatively inexpensive. When his engineering work was completed, Stout contracted with Gar Wood's truck body division to build its prototype.

The first Stout Bus from Gar Wood was completed in the spring of 1935 and tested by several Detroit area carriers in regular service. Passengers liked the modern appearance, the large interior space, and the quietness of the rear-mounted engine. The low operating cost resulting from the lightweight construction was attractive to operators. Encouraged by the bus's promising debut, Stout sought a manufacturer to put it into production.

The Dearborn Coach Company liked Stout's design but was not in a position to manufacture the buses. Dearborn Coach hired Gar Wood to build a 24-passenger model suburban bus for its company. Wood decided to put the vehicle into production and established the Motor Coach Division of Gar Wood Industries. It would use the same rear-engine, tubular space frame, all-metal construction with Ford running gear. In July 1936, the first two Gar Wood buses were delivered to the Dearborn Coach Company. The bus operations did well, and before long Ford began producing running gear especially for Gar Wood buses, designating the drivetrain as model "GWF" (Gar Wood Ford).

As a way to justify the addition of the boat division to his industrial complex, Wood announced that he would transfer the bus manufacturing operations to the Marysville boat factory. On April 6, 1938, the

Port Huron Times Herald reported, "Their plan is to adapt 30,000 square feet of floor space to accommodate the new motor coach division by the installation of overhead balcony structures which will take a large part of the boat manufacturing operations off the main floor of the plant. The addition of the balconies provides enough floor space for two complete coach assembly lines. A section of the boat division, 35 feet wide and extending the entire 500 foot length of the plant, for straight line production, has been made ready to accommodate the motor coach division."

Hancock was distressed with the plans to modify the boat factory after having its best production year ever in Marysville. Logan Wood's illness was getting worse, and he couldn't protect the boat factory as he had done so many times in the past. Hancock was on his own and had to handle the situation as best he could. It took strength of character when he publicly responded to the reporters' questions about the effect on boat production. He told them, "Our bus production will in no way affect the production of boats in the Marysville plant. No additions to the plant are planned, but it may be necessary to add office space to accommodate the office and engineering of the motor coach division." The whole idea was repugnant to Hancock and a severe blow to all the boat operation employees. They had given their very best effort to their craft, and their boats were the best in the industry. Just when it seemed that they were about to achieve the success anticipated eight years before, their superb factory was about to be shared with motor coach manufacturing.

Bill Wood, Logan's son, worked at the Marysville plant and remembers the period this way: "At that time Gar Wood Industries was building a bus from designs they purchased from William Stout who designed the Ford Tri-Motor airplane. It was rear-engined and constructed of welded steel tubing, aircraft style. The frame was welded in jigs at a Detroit Gar Wood Plant (Highland Falls), the running gear was attached, and it was then driven under its own power fifty miles to Marysville—a cold job in the winter. There the paneling was attached to the frame and they were completed for delivery." Fortunately this was the extent of the bus fabrication to take place in the boat factory. Before the complete conversion to bus production lines took place another more realistic solution was beginning to emerge.

At this time some of Gar Wood Industries' best industrial products customers began to express concern over this new interest in manufacturing motor coaches. By building this type of vehicle, they were competing directly in the same market

The finishing department was in the foreground where hardware, engines, and upholstery were installed and work was completed. Looking down the line through the open doors there were 72 boats under construction in this photo. *Gar Wood*

as the manufacturers who were their good customers. These customers felt it was not prudent for Gar Wood Industries to continue to expand its interest in building buses. When Logan Wood died in 1938, Gar Wood assumed greater responsibilities in the daily operation of the business. He was not about to create unnecessary problems. He decided that selling the motor coach division would be in his best interest. Production records for that division indicate that from 1936 to 1938 Gar Wood built 175 buses in three different model types.

In August 1939, General American Transportation Corporation of Chicago acquired the Motor Coach Division of Gar Wood Industries. Its prime activity was the manufacturing and leasing of railroad cars. The motor coach division was renamed the General American Aerocoach Company. General American was delighted to obtain the rights to this highly successful vehicle and let its customer know the plan to keep the bus essentially the same as the former Gar Wood Motor Coach. All of the company's advertisements to the trade referred to its new product as the "former Gar Wood Coach." It had an excellent reputation as a popular motor coach and General American wanted its customers to know it was still going to be the same vehicle.

With this transaction completed, the Marysville plant was returned to a total boatbuilding factory once more. Ed Hancock and the boat division employees looked forward to a new season without sharing their factory with a production line of buses.

Development of the Trophy Fleet

1930 to 1936

T he dawn of the new Marysville factory brought excitement and promise to the St. Clair River communities. Gar Wood's talented boatbuilders looked forward to working in a factory designed purposely for the types of craft they would be building. Nineteen twenty-nine had been a banner year with nearly $1.5 million in boat sales working out of the modest and cramped facilities in Algonac.

The popular 18-foot runabout made up two-thirds of the 1932 production as the trend for smaller, less expensive runabouts continued. *Chris Johnson*

Boat production started on schedule in early January with a full complement of employees eager to be part of this exciting company and proud of their new factory. Gar Wood offered three runabouts for 1930, each of which were modern, flush deck types in triple cockpit style. The runabouts were offered in 22-foot, 28-foot, and 33-foot lengths. The 22- and 28-foot runabouts were built in the new factory, and the Liberty-powered 33-foot runabout continued to be built in the Algonac facility, referred to as the "lower plant" from now on.

The system for identifying model designations was changed again for the 1930 production. Up to 1929 the 28-foot runabout was called the "Baby Gar 28." In 1929 it was called the "30" or the "40," depending on which size engine was used. The designation "30" and "40" were references to the projected top speed of the model. Model 30 was equipped with a 120-horsepower Chrysler Imperial engine (30 to 32 miles per hour), and the Model 40 was equipped with a 200-horsepower Scripps or Kermath engine (40 to 42 miles per hour). Up to 1929 the famous 33-foot runabout was known as "the Baby Gar." In 1929 the new flush deck version was introduced in midyear and officially called the Model 50 or Model 55, depending on the engine installed. The Model 50 was equipped with the 400-horsepower Gar

This view of the Model 50 provides a sense of its magnificent size and its superb detailing. These 33-footers were the last of the large standardized production runabouts and became another victim of change forced by the Depression. *Classic Boating*

Wood Liberty engine (48 to 50 miles per hour), and the Model 55 had the 500-horsepower Gar Wood Liberty (53 to 55 miles per hour).

Anticipating an additional new model in 1930, the model identification system was changed once again, but only slightly. Beginning with the 1930 models the designations became "22-30" and "22-35," "28-30," "28-35" and "28-40," and "33-50" and "33-55," referring to both the length and speed of each model. This system became necessary with the introduction of the 22-foot runabout that would have been confused with the 28-foot of the same speed. Even this improved numbering system for model identification did not allow for a large variety of models or engine options.

The production leader for Gar Wood in 1930 was the 28-foot open runabout. There were 104 built that year, some with speeds up to 55 miles per hour. This one is in the factory basin about to be water tested before delivery. *Gar Wood*

Looking back on this system it appears that Gar Wood did not foresee building such a wide range of styles and sizes of boats when he first began to name them.

The new factory was designed with special recesses in the concrete floor to facilitate the decking of 22-foot and 28-foot runabouts, which indicated a strong commitment to these two popular sizes for some time to come. Within five years the model designation system would require revision once more as the line expanded.

The 22-foot runabout was introduced in 1930 to meet the growing market for smaller boats with the same attractive styling and performance characteristics of the larger runabouts. Gar Wood achieved this objective, describing the performance of the smaller boat this way: "Swing the wheel of the twenty-two footer around, hard over, and note that she turns in her own length—without extreme listing—without soaking you and your guests. Drive back over your own wake at open throttle—and know that this boat, too, possesses the supreme Gar Wood achievement of soft-riding. And for the final test, with the boat at full speed, close the throttle. There's no tendency to plunge, she doesn't 'shovel' water ahead of her. The bow comes down slightly and gently, showing splendid trim and a smooth wake at idling speed."

In addition the 1930 sales brochure for the 22-foot runabout made a point of stating that construction and materials in this model were identical with those specified for the 28-foot and 33-foot models. Gar Wood felt that it was important for its customers to know that the smaller boats had the very same quality as the larger, more expensive model. This feature became an uncompromising characteristic of future models. Regardless of size, Gar Wood quality and attention to detail were never sacrificed.

The 28-foot runabout was a striking craft and the most popular model for 1930. From the time of its introduction in 1927, it has been one of the best-selling stock boats on the market. The beam was increased from 6 feet, 10 inches to 7 feet, 2 inches in 1928. In 1929 the hull was "completely redesigned to provide increased stability, improved planning position and greater ease of handling." Gar Wood runabouts had the widest covering boards in the industry, and this feature became a recognized design characteristic.

The alternate versions of the 28-foot runabout were models that carried the designation "sedan," "landau," and "limousine." These high-styled models were more expensive and surprisingly popular. The enclosures were handsomely designed and provided excellent ventilation. Passengers under the enclosure were treated to a quiet comfortable ride surrounded in plush red velour fabrics and soft leather upholstery. The two forward seats for the driver and companion seat were individual bucket types described as "lounge chair type, form-fitting and deeply upholstered in genuine leather."

The **sedan** top has wide permanent openings forward on each side without glass. Canvas-trimmed snap-in panels are provided to enclose these openings,

Production Volume for 1930

Stock Model/Description	Quantity	Price
Model 22-30 open runabout	41 units	$2,250
Model 22-35 open runabout	22 units	$2,650
Total 22-foot hulls	*63 units*	
Model 28-30 open runabout	38 units	$3,150
Model 28-35 open runabout	13 units	$3,600
Model 28-35 sedan	1 unit	$4,100
Model 28-40 open runabout	52 units	$4,700
Model 28-40 limousine	9 units	$5,550
Model 28-40 landau	7 units	$5,600
Model 28-55 open runabout	1 unit	$6,500
Total 28-foot hulls	*121 units*	
Model 33-50 open runabout	7 units	$8,950
Model 33-50 limousine	1 unit	$10,950
Total 33-foot hulls	*8 units*	
Model 40-foot Commuter	1 unit	$25,000
Total 40-foot hulls	*1 unit*	
Total for year:	**193 units**	

if desired. This large open area provides a more spacious feeling and facilitates docking when driving alone. In the rear quarter on each side of the enclosure are fixed-plate glass windows. The windshield is divided in the middle, and each glass panel can be raised a few inches with its own hand crank. A beautifully designed smooth sliding hatch provides easy access to the enclosed area and a snug weather seal when required. The general profile of the enclosure is similar to the limousine model.

The **limousine** top has two glass windows on each side that crank down part way, rather than the large fixed openings found on the sedan model. The ventilating windshield and aft sliding hatch on the roof are the same as the sedan. The sedan and limousine models were offered from 1928 through 1930.

The **landau** top was shown for the first time at the 1930 National Motor Boat Show. It is a permanent top with a folding rear quarter. Instead of folding down like an automobile top, the landau panel folds upward to ensure a more secure weather seal with the permanent top. The landau panel opens and closes easily, and its special feature is the large open area provided for cabin passengers if desired. The forward side windows in the enclosure crank down. The rear quarter windows are fixed and the windshield ventilates by cranking upward. This model was offered only in 1930.

The Models 33-50 and 33-55 are direct descendants of the original Baby Gars. The new model was improved and streamlined with a smartly styled flush deck and a straight line shear that provided more freeboard forward. It was a magnificent craft

This special version of the 28-foot limousine is known as the *landau*. This model was equipped with a special aft section that folds up to the cabin roof, providing unusual openness for passengers in the cabin's large bench seat. *Gar Wood*

that was enhanced by an angled folding windshield for the forward cockpit and a second one for the aft cockpit. The planing position was improved in this new model without any loss of speed or performance. The new instrument panel on the 33 boasted seven instruments. In addition to the standard five instruments, a compass and an eight-day clock were included in the indirectly lighted panel. The 33 was also available as a limousine, making it Gar Wood's top-of-the-line stock model for 1930.

The Gar Wood managers were cautiously positive as they looked ahead to 1931. They decided to offer the same three runabout models as they had for 1930. They shipped three boats to New York City for their display in the 1931 National Motor Boat Show in January—a 28-40 Landau, a 28-40 open runabout, and a 22-30 runabout. Ed Hancock worked tirelessly throughout the show with creative programs to stimulate dealers to order for the 1931 season. The high point of the show was selling a 22-35 runabout to the well-known industrial designer, Raymond Loewy of New York. Two of their best dealers, Fitzgerald and Lee of Alexandria Bay, New York, and Stearns Marine of Boston ordered three boats each. That was the full extent of the 1931 boat show results. There was some solace in that nearly every boat manufacturer had a lamentable show and many wished they had done as well as Hancock did for Gar Wood. Their arch rival, Chris-Craft, however, appeared to have a strong show boasting sales of just over $1,000,000. Before long they began to experience cancellations, and by year's end Chris-Craft lost more than $200,000 and was forced to lay off scores of employees, including two key managers, Bill MacKerer and Jack Clifford. MacKerer returned by 1935 to head Chris-Craft's design and production departments. Clifford, Chris-Craft's sales manager, was snapped up by Gar Wood to build a strong dealer organization, as he had for Chris-Craft.

Faced with inadequate orders from the New York show and a substantial inventory of new boats in the factory, there was no reason to recall the Gar Wood employees who had been laid off at the end of production in 1930. The company's key workers were assigned to build *Miss America IX* and work at the hoist factory in Detroit. The slowdown was so severe that to keep the new factory open during the winter months Ed Hancock and Charlie Jones, members of the family, stoked the boilers themselves.

Gar Wood, himself, helped out by securing an order for two boats from the Army Corps of Engineers. He also put pressure on each one of its

Production Volume for 1931		
Stock Model/Description	Quantity	Price
Model 22-30, open runabout	3 units	$2,250
Model 22-35, open runabout	8 units	$2,650
Total 22-foot hulls	*11 units*	
Model 28-35, open runabout	4 units	$3,600
Model 28-40, open runabout	11 units	$4,700
Model 28-55, open runabout	4 units	$7,500
Total 28-foot hulls	*19 units*	
Model 33-50, open runabout	2 units	$8,950
Total 33-foot hulls	*2 units*	
Total for year:	**32 units**	

suppliers of marine products to sponsor major display ads featuring Gar Wood Boats along with the supplier's own products. In March 1931 Gar Wood set two new world speed records in *Miss America IX*, which continued to keep his name in front of the public. The power and influence of Gar Wood's name carried tremendous influence for marine dealers and their customers. Even with all of this, the boat business struggled.

The year 1931 was one of the low points in Gar Wood production history. It is estimated that more than half of the 32 boats delivered that season were from the previous year's production. Further evidence of dealers' desperation is that all the 1931 boats were delivered during May, June, and July, a strong indication that dealers were making sure the new boats were sold before arranging delivery. Dealers were not taking any chance of tying up their limited resources for stock inventory.

Ed Hancock prudently listened to the suggestions from dealers attending the New York show. They reported that their customers admired the big Gar Wood runabouts, but they were more at ease operating smaller boats. This was especially true for first-time boaters. Dealers on smaller lakes and sheltered rivers also expressed a preference toward smaller boats without sacrificing Gar Wood quality and performance. It appeared that dealers would be willing to stock two smaller boats rather than take a chance on one large runabout.

The challenge for George Joachim was to design and build a new runabout that was better suited to the dealers' needs but would still get Mr. Wood's endorsement. The first two years in the "world's

The magnificent Model 33-50 limousine is speeding along at 48 miles per hour. It was the only example of this model built in 1930 as the era of big runabouts and big limousines was about to end. *Gar Wood*

finest boat factory" had not been exactly what the boss had in mind when he decided to build it.

Wood had new priorities on his mind. *Miss America X*, the ultimate Harmsworth hydroplane, was under construction at the lower plant in Algonac. The Marysville factory was now called the "upper plant" by workers who frequently traveled between the two locations. The Detroit Yacht Club once again hosted the Harmsworth Trophy Race in the summer of 1932. This meant that finishing and testing the new defender was the primary concern in Algonac.

In September 1931 George Joachim proposed two new models for the company's 1932 line, an 18-foot runabout and a 25-foot runabout, hoping to stimulate sales and to respond to dealers' suggestions. Wood quickly reviewed the designs, made a few suggestions, and told Joachim to go ahead with a prototype of each model for water testing. If they tested well, Wood wanted the new models ready for the January 1932 National Motor Boat Show in New York City. Once again, Wood focused his full attention on the development of *Miss America X*.

Joachim and his crew were eager for the opportunity to create these two new models. They believed the new boats would get strong support from their dealers. Ed Hancock devised a subtle strategy to make it appear that production was moving ahead.

By skipping ahead on assigned hull numbers 3199 to 4100 it gave the appearance of more production to their dealers. It was a ploy to motivate dealers who all knew that Gar Wood hulls were numbered consecutively. This little "adjustment" of hull numbers might encourage dealer confidence that boats were moving better than they thought. It was a desperate time, and everyone did whatever possible to improve his or her situation.

The two new models were completed by mid-October and tested extremely well in every phase of operation. They were particularly pleased with the performance of the small 18-footer on which their hopes were built. The results were so good that Jack Clifford, the new sales manager fresh from Chris-Craft, prepared an unusual full-page advertisement in *Motor Boating* magazine stating, "This is the season when production in the boat-building industry slackens to a snail's pace. At the Gar Wood plant, the whine of the band-saw and planer is stilled, and a quieter, but none-the-less important activity replaces the bustle and clatter of men and machinery. The drawing board and the T-square are the center of interest. Plans are afoot for 1932.

"Gar Wood, Incorporated, views the coming year with optimism and confidence. Gar Wood runabouts for 1932 again will be built to merit a position of

The 1932 18-foot runabout was the first standardized Gar Wood runabout without three cockpits. This downsized model was aimed at first-time buyers with a desire for quality on a modest budget. *John Clark*

leadership in quality and value. Present models will be improved and refined wherever possible. In addition, two new models are under construction, and will have completed their initial tests by the time this message appears.

"As a consequence, Gar Wood dealers will continue to enjoy the advantages they always have had— plus the opportunity of reaching a larger market through an augmented line that will afford broader coverage."

This ad was an unprecedented printed statement to the boating world and, in particular, to dealers. It made it clear that the actual building of boats was a *seasonal* activity even at Gar Wood's new factory. The ad declared that Gar Wood was moving ahead with "optimism and confidence," a clear acknowledgment of the slower sales the company had been experiencing along with a message of encouragement to its dealers. But ever more important was the advanced announcement of two new models even before they had been water tested, demonstrating that Gar Wood was listening to the suggestions of its dealers by augmenting its boat line to include smaller craft.

Gar Wood's display in the 1932 National Motor Boat Show included a 28-40 runabout, which always attracted a crowd, and two new models, the 18-35

dual cockpit runabout and the 25-45 triple cockpit runabout. Gar Wood's 18-footer was an excellent design with wide covering boards, flared hull, formal cut water, substantial freeboard, and generous beam. It was a very attractive, high-quality small runabout that could hold its own among the larger, more expensive runabouts. Although this boat was small, it retained all of the attractive Gar Wood qualities.

The new models pleased the dealers, and several 18-footers were ordered at the show for early spring delivery. There was a feeling of success in the Gar Wood camp and a feeling that this year might be the turning point for sales and production.

America hosted the 1932 Olympic summer games in Los Angeles and the winter events in Lake Placid. Olympic sports were on the minds of most Americans and Gar Wood joined in the competitive spirit by successfully defending his Harmsworth Trophy in spectacular fashion. The races attracted record crowds of nearly a half million spectators lining the shores of the St. Clair River to get a glimpse of the world's fastest race boats. In these harsh economic times Wood's genius to create fabulous race boats and drive them himself to victory gave people all over the nation something to feel good about. He was as great a hero to most Americans as any Olympic gold

medalist. Gar Wood's name was the most recognized and respected in boating, and by continuing to create and race spectacular boats, he symbolized the financial success that was still achievable in America.

In spite of weak boat sales for the third straight year, Wood was determined not to abandon the boat business that carried his name. The boats his company built were the best in the industry, and his financial position was secure enough that he knew he could personally keep the boat company in operation until the economic climate for boats improved. He also was stubborn enough not to give up and was determined to keep his boat company operating as long as his former partner and rival, Chris Smith, continued to stay in business. Chris-Craft lost over a quarter of a million dollars in 1932.

Wood continued to prevail on every major supplier to feature Gar Wood Boats in the company's regular advertising with copy prepared by Jack Clifford. He was a powerful figure and his influence produced quick results. Champion Spark Plugs, Gray Marine Engine Company, Anaconda Copper, Scripps Engines, Texaco, Bakelite, Duplex Oil, and Chrysler Marine all ran attractive advertisements featuring Gar Wood Boats in a variety of major magazines in 1932. Wood was determined to succeed with his line of boats even as the nation's economic slump forced other boatbuilders to close down. Nineteen thirty-two was the first year that Gar Wood did not ship any of its new production overseas. Foreign sales had always been a prestigious factor in the company's marketing strategy, and the total loss of foreign sales was another indicator of the extent of the shrinking consumer base.

Wood's commitment to keep the boat factory open was severely tested in 1933. The company was encouraged by the impressive acceptance of the 18-foot runabout series and felt that there was a good market for the new 25-foot runabout. Although there was a noticeable trend toward smaller, less expensive boats, Wood decided not to introduce any additional new models at this time. Nevertheless, he directed George Joachim to explore new design ideas, including a 16-foot model. Those at Gar Wood were well aware that Chris-Craft had introduced its 15 1/2-foot runabout midway through 1931, and it was considered a sales success, although not very profitable. In late 1932 Chris-Craft introduced its first "utility" model, a stripped-down version of its 24-foot runabout, as Chris-Craft explored new ways to entice buyers with less expensive, all-purpose craft.

Wood determined that it was time to close his New York branch and decided to pass up the 1933 National Motor Boat Show. All four 28-40 runabouts sold in 1933 were actually built in 1932's production. Hull numbers were, once again, jumped forward from 4299 to 5200 to give dealers the illusion of greater production volume.

President Franklin D. Roosevelt promised Americans a New Deal, bringing new vigor and energy to the White House and seeking ways to end the Depression that hung over the nation's economy. Gar Wood and his *Miss America X* received another formal challenge from England to defend the Harmsworth Trophy in 1933. This time Hubert Scott Paine went after the trophy in *Miss Britain*. Prohibition in America was finally repealed, and Chicago was the host city for 22 million people attending the World's Fair saluting "A Century of Progress."

It was another great Harmsworth victory for Wood, and the joy of his successful defense helped take some of the sting away from the dismal sales results for 1933.

Production Volume for 1932

Stock Model	Quantity	Price
Model 18-30	15 units	$1,200
Model 18-35	28 units	$1,400
Total 18-foot hulls	*43*	
Model 22-30	2 units	$2,250
Model 22-35	3 units	$2,600
Total 22-foot hulls	*5*	
Model 25-30	1 unit	$3,150
Model 25-35	2 units	$3,450
Model 25-45	5 units	$4,450
Model 25 hull only	1 unit	
Total 25-foot hulls	*9*	
Model 28-40	3 units	$4,975
Model 28-55	4 units	$6,500
Total 28-foot hulls	*7*	
Total for year:	**64 units**	

There was only one question on everyone's mind at the Marysville factory: Could it possibly get any worse? Five years before, in 1929 they had built 224 boats, and now their production was off by almost 90 percent. In 1929 this talented team of boatbuilders could build 24 boats in a month under the most crowded working conditions in Algonac. Four years later in a superb new factory 24 boats would be the entire year's volume. For employees at the state-of-the-art plant, it was an unimaginable situation.

Chris-Craft and Gar Wood employees were often neighbors in this small boatbuilding community and knew everything about each other's business. In 1933 Chris-Craft lost another $250,000, making its

continued on page 76

Production Volume for 1933

Stock Model	Quantity	Price
Model 18-30	2 units	$1,200
Model 18-35	14 units	$1,400
Model 18-40	1 unit	$1,750
Total 18-foot hulls	*17*	
Model 25-35	1 unit	$3,150
Model 25-45	2 units	$4,475
Total 25-foot hulls	*3*	
Model 28-40	4 units	$4,975
Total 28-foot hulls	*4*	
Total for year:	**24 units**	

The 1934 18-foot Special Runabout was an important design milestone for this length boat. It was this model that successfully moved the rear cockpit ahead of the engine without sacrificing performance. *Jim Brown*

Windshield Styling

Perhaps the most distinguishing embellishment for any small craft is the windshield. It is both functional and a unique enhancement on which classic boaters place great value. Gar Wood understood the importance of an attractive windshield better than its contemporaries and made its windshields bold, handsome, and dashing. By 1932 the company's entire line of runabouts featured V-windshields with most of them completely framed in heavy chrome and folding for added enjoyment. Even the utility models were given special attention, so that their unique windshields were proportional to their larger hulls and were in perfect harmony with the total design configuration of the boat. This attention to superb windshield design was applied to the streamline cabin utility models and cruisers. Here are some samples of Gar Wood's windshield artistry.

A 1930 28-foot runabout.

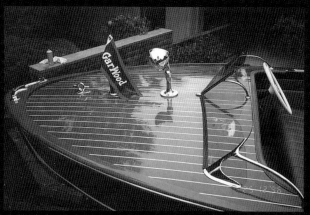

A 1946 18-foot, 6-inch utility.

A 1939 20-foot, 6-inch Streamline sedan.

The aft cockpit of a 1930 28-foot Laudau.

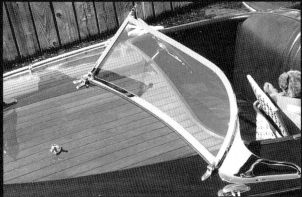

A 1941 19-foot, 6-inch runabout.

A 1940 24-foot, 6-inch Custom utility.

A 1937 24-foot Custom utility.

A 1929 28-foot Baby Gar runabout.

A 1928 33-foot Baby Gar runabout.

A 1936 28-foot runabout (folded).

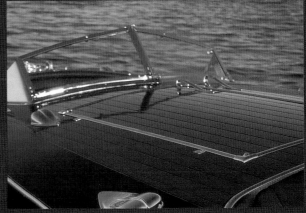

A 1936 28-foot runabout (aft).

A 1926 33-foot Baby Gar runabout.

Gar Wood continued to downsize its models to attract new buyers. By 1934 the most popular model in the fleet was the 16-foot runabout at $895, keeping the company in business during a perilous economic time. *Chris Johnson*

Continued from page 71

cumulative losses over the past three years in excess of $700,000. Those who had jobs were grateful but wondered how much longer their boatbuilding activities could last for an employer that was not making a profit.

Remarkably, it was Wood who expressed confidence and optimism this time. His industrial sales had been climbing steadily, and he was convinced that the worst was over and that as consumer confi-

dence returned, boat sales would certainly begin to climb. He predicted that 1934 would be a good year for the boat company. When President Roosevelt devalued the dollar to 60 cents, Wood instructed Jack Clifford to recapture the export market. Foreign sales since 1925 had been a valuable segment of the business. There were no overseas shipments of Gar Wood Boats in either 1932 or 1933 due to the weaker European currency. Devaluation of the dollar could open this market once more.

Wood and his key men had ample time to test several new models and decided on a 16-foot split cockpit runabout and a new version of the 18-foot runabout they called the "Special" for production. The 18-foot Special used the same basic hull as the current 18-foot runabout. It was given an attractive folding-V windshield, and the rear cockpit was moved forward of the engine compartment. The dual cockpits forward in such a small runabout made a styling statement that influenced every other builder. By moving the second cockpit forward, it became larger, drier, closer to other passengers and provided a better riding angle by moving the passenger weight forward. It was a groundbreaking design and a sweet riding craft. Since the standard 18-foot runabout had been quite popular, it was decided to

The darling of the 1934 fleet was the famous 16-foot Speedster. A spectacular performer, the Speedster always drew everyone's attention. The Speedster is still one of Gar Wood's most sought-after models. *Jim Brown*

continue to offer it without modification along with the new Special version. This decision meant that Gar Wood would offer two different versions of the 18-foot runabout in the same production year.

The introduction of the 16-foot runabout was the new secret weapon in Gar Wood's renewed assault on sluggish sales. Wood wanted a boat that was classy, attractive, fast, and most of all, affordable to anyone interested in owning a quality boat. Their ads would describe it this way:

> Only 16 feet overall with a speed of 34 miles; that's the new Gar Wood runabout model 16-35, typically Gar Wood in every detail from stem to stern. It is roomy enough for five. Rides with the utmost comfort. Is perfectly sea worthy in any water. The exquisite blending of the hand finished African mahogany V-type hull with rich leather upholstery, the chromium plated deck fittings and metal trim, the shatterproof glass windshield and the marine type instrument panel, denote painstaking care of construction and good taste in appointments. In performance and handling the new Gar Wood 16-35 upholds the Gar Wood reputation of excellence. It is an ideal small boat in every respect and the greatest value ever offered in the low price class.

Of course, the real message to potential buyers was in the price—$895! This was a strong attraction to buyers who wanted Gar Wood quality. This boat included all the nice features—African mahogany, chrome hardware, genuine leather upholstery, and Chrysler power—at a price that was in reach of more buyers. Once again Gar Wood was able to design a small runabout that did not compromise quality or performance. Other builders offered low-priced 16-footers that cut every corner in design, materials, and construction to keep the price low, and the boats conveyed that message clearly in their appearance. Wood's 16-footer was no compromise; the question was, would the public accept it?

The 16-footer and the Special 18-footer were well received and the return of the export business accounted for nearly one-third of sales, which reached 141 units by the end of July. It looked like their faith had finally been rewarded and there would be prospects for a future for the Marysville factory.

There was much to be happy about during the 1934 season. Dealers were pleased with everything about the new models and especially aware that Gar Wood had listened to their suggestions. Wood's determination to keep his boat operation in place during such a difficult period fostered even stronger dealer loyalty and provided confidence as they entered a new era together. Gar Wood Boats were shipped to overseas dealers in 12 foreign countries, including

The abundant room available in the 20-foot utility model made it immediately popular with boaters who needed a boat that was more versatile than a runabout. *Bob Cunningham*

first-time sales in China, Algiers, Spain, France, Brazil, The Netherlands, and Switzerland. This was a very good indicator of the value of Gar Wood's worldwide name recognition secured through his racing achievements. It also suggested the easing of economic struggles in overseas countries.

Overseas sales were a big boost, and Gar Wood employees were hopeful that this market would continue to grow. No one could imagine the consequences of events in Germany that made Adolph Hitler both chancellor and president. In America economic recovery seemed finally to be within reach, and the situation in Germany seemed a distant concern.

Production Volume for 1934

Stock Model	Quantity	Price
Model 18-30	10 units	$1,300
Model 18-30S	6 units	$1,300
Model 18-35	17 units	$1,500
Model 18-35S	16 units	$1,500
Total 18-foot hulls	*49 units*	
Model 16-35	91 units	$ 895
Model 16 Speedster	1 unit	$1,195
Total 16-foot hulls	*92 units*	
Model 33-50 open	1 unit	$8,975
Total 33-foot hulls	*1 unit*	
Total for year:	**142 units**	

It was toward the end of production in 1934 that another experimental design was completed. It was a variation of the new 16-footer with controls in the aft cockpit and the forward cockpit decked over. There was just room for two in this sporty new design that Gar's brother Phil took as his own so he could more fully test it. The prototype was dubbed the "Speedster" and the name stuck. A group of gentlemen from the Thousand Islands read about the new craft in a feature story in *Motor Boating* and thought it would be the perfect boat to bring sport racing back to their area of the St. Lawrence River. In the same issue they read the first ad to appear on the Speedster:

> Boy! What a boat . . . what speed . . . what a thrill . . . Sixteen feet of glistening mahogany, chromium plate, and genuine leather; every inch typically Gar Wood. . . . It's one of the smartest, speediest small boats of the Gar Wood line. . . . Sit at the wheel; press the starter; its husky, 92 horse power, 6 cylinder Chrysler engine awakes, eager to respond to your moods. . . . Advance the throttle and the water slips under you at a dizzy speed of 40 miles. . . . The wind whistles through your hair and sings in your ears a melody of the great out doors; moments seem like hours of contentment in the sheer joy of living. . . . It's the small speedboat you've been wanting; the New Gar Wood contribution to lovers of motor boating. Make up your mind right now to own a new Gar Wood SPEEDSTER.

How could anyone resist an ad like this? Five gentlemen agreed it would be great fun to have a fleet of Speedsters shipped to Alexandria Bay, New York, for the 1935 season. They placed their order with Fitzgerald and Lee, Gar Wood's number one dealer, and brought the return of sport racing to the Thousand Islands.

Filled with a new level of confidence Wood decided to expand his fleet for 1935. It was time to introduce an attractive all-purpose, smartly styled boat to the fleet. Once again by listening to the dealers, Wood learned of growing interest in a boat that would serve family interests better than the sporty looking runabouts that might be built for less than a similar size runabout. The company's rivals at Chris-Craft had experimented with a type of "open" runabout in 1932–33. They referred to this as a "utility" boat, and the name seemed to fit. Gar Wood's designers felt that the Chris-Craft interpretation was too austere and resembled a work boat. Gar Wood's 20-foot utility would be attractive, comfortable, and provide seats for nine on genuine leather upholstery. The open interior of the utility was lined in varnished mahogany planking. Once again Gar Wood made its version of the utility several steps above its competition in appointments, engine options, and performance, always seeking the more discriminating buyer.

In 1936 Gar Wood introduced the 20-foot cabin utility. It was an instant success and surprisingly outsold the 20-foot open utility model. *Classic Boating*

Wood's designers also felt that it was time to build a small family cruiser. This decision would take Gar Wood directly into a market area that Chris-Craft had successfully developed some years before. Wood started with a 26-foot cruiser. It would provide a family of four with an attractive boat at an affordable price that was much nicer than the 25-foot Utility Cruiser that Chris-Craft offered. Gar Wood offered an unusual range of options, including varnished hulls and twin engines. A great promotional story appeared in *Motor Boating* magazine when a well-to-do Algerian purchased a special 26-foot Cruiser for delivery in Africa. Gar Wood sold a surprising 26 of these popular family cruisers in 1935.

With the prospects of a serious challenge for the Harmsworth Trophy fading more each year, Wood devoted more time to the activities of the boat business and, in particular, their new models. George Joachim was still fully involved in creating the new designs, but Wood was there frequently to make suggestions. Often Wood would hop into his Fairchild Amphibian in Detroit and fly to Marysville, land in the river, and taxi his plane to the shore of the factory property. He loved to fly and would take advantage of any reason to get in his plane to check on "some detail" at either of the boat factories.

Inspired by the success of the 1934 sales volume, Gar Wood announced that it would exhibit eight different models in the 1935 National Motor Boat Show. The announcement declared that "three of these models are entirely new, never before publicly displayed." The three new models were the 26-foot cruiser, the 20-foot utility, and the 16-foot Speedster, each one a radical departure from traditional Gar Wood products. An editorial footnote continued, stating, "The models are new in conception and design and beautiful examples of the high quality workmanship that distinguishes the Gar Wood line."

The economic recovery continued to strengthen through 1935. The beautiful new French ocean-liner, *Normandie*, won the Blue Riband for crossing the Atlantic in record time with an average speed of 29.7 knots. Sir Malcolm Campbell beat his own land speed record in Salt Flats, Utah, traveling 301 miles per hour, and aviator Howard Hughes traveled 351 miles per hour to set a new air speed mark. Kodak introduced Kodachrome as the first color film for home photography, and Douglas Aircraft introduced the venerable DC-3, which became the backbone of the air transportation industry. President Roosevelt fulfilled a campaign promise by enacting Social Security, providing comprehensive care for elderly,

Production Volume for 1935		
Stock Model	**Quantity**	**Price**
Model 16-35, open runabout	31 units	$ 995
Model 16 Speedster	9 units	$1,195
Total 16-foot hulls	*40*	
Model 18-30, open runabout	1 unit	$1,300
Model 18-30S, open runabout	3 units	$1,300
Model 18-35, open runabout	9 units	$1,500
Model 18-35S, open runabout	12 units	$1,500
Total 18-foot hulls	*25*	
Model 22-30, open runabout	6 units	$2,100
Model 22-35, open runabout	5 units	$2,400
Model 22-45, open runabout	1 unit	$3,400
Model 22, hull only	1 unit	
Total 22-foot hulls	*13*	
Model 28-40, open runabout	2 units	$4,975
Model 28-40, landau	1 unit	$5,750
Model 28-55, open runabout	1 unit	$6,500
Model 28, hull only	1 unit	
Total 28-foot hulls	*5*	
Model 20-foot utility	33 units	$1,195
Total 20-foot hulls	*33*	
Model 26-foot cruiser	26 units	$2,500
Total 26-foot hulls	*26*	
Total for year:	**142 units**	

handicapped, and unemployed Americans. Germany and Japan increased their aggressiveness in Europe and Asia, casting an uneasy shadow over the recovery efforts.

Although the number of units produced in 1935 was nearly identical to 1934, there was a marked increase in total sales revenue. The variety of new boats sold in 1935 was significantly more expensive than the models that were sold in 1934, producing a 40 percent increase in total revenue. As Hancock and Clifford studied the national economic recovery process as it related to their product line of boats, there was a discernible trend toward new types of boats, such as utilities and more luxurious models.

In 1935 Wood accomplished a remarkable media feat. His good friend George Reis, the well-known 1934 Gold Cup champion from Lake George, New York, wrote a 12-page article that appeared in the 1935 Boat Show Issue of *Motor Boating* magazine under the title, "Behind the Scenes with Gar Wood."

It began as an interesting visit with Gar Wood at his Marysville factory but soon became a commercial tour of the facilities and the products used by Wood's employees to build their boats. The article featured 18 appealing photographs and was skillfully written; however, the readers soon realized that the text of the article was a disguised commercial promotion for Gar Wood Boats and the various manufacturers that supplied products and services to Gar Wood. It may be the first undocumented "infomercial" on record. The article proceeded to identify 28 manufacturers by name and some 36 specific products that were used by Gar Wood. Each product was praised for its superior quality and its contribution to Gar Wood's outstanding reputation as a boatbuilder. Chris Smith must have nearly swallowed his cigar when he read this "article" in his favorite magazine.

Later that year another feature article reviewed a special version of Gar Wood's new 26-foot Cruiser that was being shipped to a "prominent" Algerian living in Africa. The story pointed out the worldwide interest in Gar Wood Boats and the expansion of the company's line to include cruisers that by all accounts were attracting international buyers. Gar Wood enjoyed a great deal of free promotional reporting and was skilled at arranging it.

Gar Wood Industries was doing well, and Wood was confident that boat production would continue to grow. To kick off the 1936 season his ads were filled with positive headlines like, "A Thundering Salute to a Re-awakened Boating World!"

The editorial coverage in the magazines expressed excitement about Gar Wood's expanded line of boats. One editor wrote glowingly about the new attitude:

Casting his weather eye over the boating horizon, with much the same keen interest with which he has scanned the Harmsworth race course on seven thrill filled occasions, Gar Wood, the boating world's number one racing man, sees a tremendous increase in boating activity during 1936.

It's easy to see the advanced styling touch of Gar Wood's designers in this 32-foot express cruiser for 1936. With speeds to 35 miles per hour this boat provided Gar Wood's rivals with a new standard of excellence in cruiser design.

With the storm of depression far astern, the boating industry now looks ahead to a long period of good weather and improved selling conditions. The boating world has emerged from the shallows and is again headed for open water and sunny skies.

Sensing this shift in economic winds some time ago, Gar Wood, Inc., has for months been preparing the greatest boat show exhibit ever to carry the Gar Wood name.

Gar Wood's 1936 fleet will be known as the Trophy Fleet—and with seven Harmsworth victories as a background—no fleet of motor boats could be more fittingly named. The fleet will include 69 magnificent models under the command of a new 32 foot streamline, custom cruiser flagship.

By 1936 Gar Wood's international sales increased substantially. Here two new Gar Wood models are displayed in the showroom of Ronstrom and Bahrne, Gar Wood's Stockholm, Sweden, dealership.

Gar Wood was getting more involved in the boat business. The new 32-footer was designed as an attractive express cruiser and fishing boat that Wood, himself, would use at his winter home in Florida. It was a smart, modern design that was the best looking stock express cruiser offered by any builder in 1936. Its styling was so refreshing that it influenced other builders, including Chris-Craft, to incorporate its design features. There were 10 engine options with speeds to 35 miles per hour. The interior was all-natural African mahogany with luxurious accommodations for six. Standard equipment included spotlight, military mast, Philco radio, and beveled glass mirrors. One of the first 32-foot Express Cruisers was sold to General Jorge Ubico, president of Guatemala, with twin Scripps 202s providing speeds to 35 miles per hour.

One of the other new offerings for 1936 was the 20-foot Streamline Cabin Utility. This model shared the same hull as the popular 20-foot utility with an attractive cabin enclosure over the two forward seats. It offered a ventilating V-type windshield and two opening glass windows on each side of the cabin. The back of the cabin has a roll-down curtain to fully enclose the cabin. Providing a good-looking cabin enclosure on the utility boat turned out to be a popular concept, and Gar Wood's designers did a superb job making theirs more attractive than Chris-Craft's versions. The 20-foot Streamline Cabin Utility

turned out to be Gar Wood's most popular model for 1936 with 45 units sold.

By 1936 Gar Wood offered 13 models from which their customers could select 67 variations. At this point, however, both Gar Wood and Chris-Craft had adopted the practice of calling each engine option in the same hull a particular *model*. Thus, in 1936 Gar Wood announced "the greatest fleet in boating history," made up of 67 models. Identifying models in this way inflated the boat maker's production image and made for very impressive advertising. It soon became the standard way for boatbuilders to promote their offerings to dealers and their customers. In many cases models were carried in the catalog listings and never actually delivered because no one ordered the particular engine option that constituted that model number.

This technique also made it necessary for Gar Wood to introduce a new system to identify its various models. It would be the fourth model identification system in eight years. The first digit in the model code would identify the production year and the next two digits the style and engine option. All models built in 1936 would begin with the digit 6, all those built in 1937 would begin with 7, and so on.

By May 1936 Ed Hancock reported, "Everything points to a record-breaking year. January and February shipments were 233% ahead of those of the

Production Volume for 1936

Model	Description	Engine, cylinder horsepower	Quantity	Price
600	16-foot Runabout	GW Kermath 4-56	1 unit	$1,070
601	16-foot Runabout	Chrysler Ace 6-73	29 units	$1,195
601sp	16-foot Runabout	Gray 6-225	1 unit	$1,595
602	16-foot Runabout	Gray 6-103	5 units	$1,375
606	16-foot Speedster	Gray 6-125	1 unit	$1,525
613	18-foot Runabout	Gray 6-125	3 units	$1,850
615	18-foot Sp. Rnbt.	GW Kermath 4-56	1 unit	$1,450
616	18-foot Sp. Rnbt.	Chrysler Ace 6-73	7 units	$1,575
617	18-foot Sp. Rnbt.	Chrysler Crown 6-93	14 units	$1,775
617G	18-foot Sp. Rnbt.	Gray 6-103	1 unit	$1,775
618	18-foot Sp. Rnbt.	Gray 6-125	1 unit	$1,905
620	22-foot Runabout	Chrysler Crown 6-93	2 units	$2,175
621	22-foot Runabout	Chrysler Royal 8-115	6 units	$2,475
622	22-foot Runabout	Chrysler Majestic 8-152	2 units	$2,775
623	22-foot Runabout	Scripps 152 6-169	3 units	$3,475
624	22-foot Runabout	Pr. GW Kermath 4-56	1 unit	$3,275
631	25-foot Runabout	Chrysler Majestic 8-152	1 unit	$3,275
640	28-foot Runabout	Scripps 202 6-212	3 units	$4,975
641	28-foot Runabout	Scripps 300 12-316	2 units	$6,500
660	18-foot Utility	GW Kermath 4-56	13 units	$1,095
661	18-foot Utility	Chrysler Ace 6-73	8 units	$1,220
662	18-foot Utility	Chrysler Crown 6-93	2 units	$1,420
665	20-foot Utility	GW Kermath 4-56	3 units	$1,195
666	20-foot Utility	Chrysler Ace 6-73	20 units	$1,320
667	20-foot Utility	Chrysler Crown 6-93	7 units	$1,520
670	20-foot Cabin Utility	Chrysler Ace 6-73	20 units	$1,570
671	20-foot Cabin Utility	Chrysler Crown 6-93	13 units	$1,770
672	20-foot Cabin Utility	Chrysler Royal 8-115	2 units	$2,070
681	26-foot Cruiser	Chrysler Ace 6-73 RG	3 units	$2,995
682	26-foot Cruiser	Chrysler Crown RG	3 units	$3,395
687	26-foot Cruiser	Pr. Gray 6-125	1 unit	$4,600
696	32-foot Ex. Cr.	Pr. Chrysler Ace 6-73	2 units	$7,800
697	32-foot Ex. Cr.	Pr. Chrysler Crown 6-93	1 unit	$8,200
699	32-foot Ex. Cr.	Pr. Scripps 202 6-212	1 unit	$10,900

Total production for 1936: 183 units

first two months of last year. Dealer applications, which are accurate indicators of increased interest in boating, are running ahead of any similar period."

Everyone at Gar Wood could feel new momentum at the boat factory. The company was now offering a full line of stock models from 16-foot Speedsters to 32-foot luxury Express Cruisers. It had a variety of boats to satisfy a wide range of buyers, and its dealer network was growing steadily. The workers liked the "Trophy Fleet" and felt that they had developed a valuable niche in the boat-building industry for which the future would be good. They were proud craftsmen who were beginning to enjoy the feeling of pride and security, once again, that comes with building the very best your craft has to offer.

On an early morning in Miami, Gar Wood and Orlin Johnson prepare to make history in *Miss America IX* by being the first to officially exceed 100 miles per hour over a measured mile. It was one of Wood's most cherished accomplishments.

Achieving Design Perfection

1937 to 1941

Convinced that the worst economic problems were behind them, Gar Wood kicked off 1937 by printing a large, attractive catalog describing its new Trophy Fleet models. The 26-page catalog, with a full-color cover and 48 photographs, announced 125 custom-built models. It was an impressive piece of advertising that described the many features of the efficient boat factory, construction specifications, and details of

The 28-foot custom runabout was the *Flagship* of the 1941 Gar Wood Trophy Fleet. This model is considered the pinnacle of design achievement in the field of triple cockpit runabouts. *Classic Boating* each model. It also included a special message from Gar Wood.

The national ads boldly claimed that its 58 models of runabouts and 36 models of utilities were the largest in the industry. There was a renewed spirit among the workers in the Marysville plant. New boat orders at the New York show were excellent, and there were signs of a very productive year ahead.

In Detroit several General Motors plants had been shut down for several weeks by "sit down" strikes in which the workers gained nearly all their demands. It wasn't long before a small group of United Auto Workers convinced a core of Chris-Craft employees of the benefits of organizing a union. By mid-March employee unrest led to a strike at Chris-Craft that halted production and put 600 workers off the job. The timing of the strike hurt deliveries to anxious dealers at a critical time and further harmed the deteriorating relations between the Smith family and its employees. The results of the strike continued to distance the Smiths from the Algonac community.

In Marysville Gar Wood was expanding on the sales success of the 20-foot utility and the 20-foot cabin utility during the prior year and decided to introduce a larger, more deluxe, 24-foot utility model in both open and cabin styles. The dealers suggested a cabin version for the 18-foot utility model. There was a customer preference for the room and flexibility of the utility style along with attractive styling, luxury appointments, and good performance.

Gar Wood literature described the new 24-foot utility this way: "There has been a demand and a very definite demand that Gar Wood build a big, beautiful, roomy, utility boat with cruiser comfort and smoothness . . . more seating room, more storage and tackle space, more luggage and more food . . . more of everything . . . more beam (7'-7"), more freeboard (3'-9") and more motor options (fourteen including twin engines) with speeds to 42 miles per hour. There is a large ice box built into the back of the front seat and a full folding windshield."

This big utility made a strong impact on the market that would immediately be felt by rival

In 1937 Gar Wood introduced the 24-foot Custom utility to the boating world. This upscale version of a general-purpose craft provided a new level of luxury and status to this emerging class. *Magri*

Chris-Craft. The competition between the two boat-building firms was growing more intense, and Chris-Craft answered with its own 24-foot utility called the "Sportsman." The Sportsman was a surprisingly upscale boat for Chris-Craft and was its only utility to use leather upholstery. The company decided not to include an aft seat, a fold-down windshield, or the built-in icebox that Gar Wood offered on its 24-foot deluxe utility.

The enclosed version of the 24-foot utility was a magnificent craft that included all of the features of the open utility model plus a standard toilet under the amidships seat, roll-down windows in the cabin, eight lockers, and a removable rear seat. Gar Wood's 18-foot cabin utility had snap-in curtains rather than glass in the side openings, which was a practical enclosure method for the smaller boat. The cabin version proved to be even more popular than the open version and outsold it by three-to-one.

The original split cockpit model of the 18-foot runabout was discontinued. The 18-foot Special runabout was available only through 1936, then that too was discontinued. The new 19-foot Custom runabout model replaced both 18-footers. The 19-footer provided superior performance, a larger cockpit, and a much better ride than its 18-foot predecessors. Its dimensions were significantly larger all around with added beam, greater freeboard, abundant flare, and a partially barreled transom. Offering speeds to 39 miles per hour, this model scooped the industry and was without equal in its debut at the 1937 National Motor Boat Show.

Clifford, Hancock, and Joachim all believed that the variety of models that were currently being built suited their facilities and their dealers' needs perfectly. They decided to focus their attention on improved styling and firmly establishing themselves as the clear leaders in this particular realm of the boating market. Business continued to improve, and 1937 turned out to be the most productive year ever in Marysville with 267 new boats delivered. After eight full years in the Marysville factory, they finally outproduced the 1929 record volume of the old Algonac factory.

The most popular boat in the 1937 Trophy Fleet turned out to be the 20-foot Streamline Cabin Utility that was a pleasant surprise to everyone. Cabin utility models accounted for 40 percent of the total production. When combined with the open models the utility models represented nearly 60 percent of the 1937 production. This data was fascinating when considering the utility was only in production since 1935 and the cabin utility since 1936. Gar Wood had a special advantage over its competition since no

Gar Wood owned 11 airplanes, and this Fairchild A-942-B Amphibian was one of his favorites. He often flew in this airplane from Detroit to his boat factory in Marysville, where this photo was taken by one of his employees. *Bill Lester*

other builder had such a variety of handsome cabin utilities in its standard production.

Nineteen thirty-seven began with promise but ended in disappointment. In Detroit a young boxer named Joe Lewis beat Jim Braddock in eight rounds to win the world's heavyweight crown and give Detroit's citizens a hometown champion. The dirigible *Hindenberg* crossed the Atlantic but blew up in New Jersey, and Europe edged closer to war. The U. S. census of 1937 showed that there were still eight million jobless workers in America (out of a total population of 130 million). Logan Wood fell seriously ill and in his absence Gar Wood Industries made a questionable decision to move its new bus division to the Marysville boat factory, where it would share production space with the boatbuilders.

The plan to move the bus division was a money-saving decision that showed the corporate disregard for the welfare of the boat division just when it appeared that the boat business was about to flourish. Even though news releases announced this decision and the Marysville factory was renovated to accommodate the fabrication of the Gar Wood buses, the bus division was sold before total modifications of the boat factory were completed. The announcement and the renovations of the boat factory created major disruptions so that boat production in 1938 dropped to one-third of its 1937 volume.

The decision to build buses in the boat factory just as it was beginning to show the promise so long anticipated was an example of the corporate confusion that prevailed in Logan's absence. Gar Wood began selling his corporate common stock in 1936 as his brother Logan's health declined, and Gar desired to convert his assets into a more liquid state. Logan's health continued to fail and in 1938 he died. The corporate treasurer, Glen Bassett, became the new president of Gar Wood Industries. In his former position as treasurer, Bassett must have been well aware of the boat division's difficulties in meeting its financial obligations, let alone making a profit. As leader of the whole operation, Bassett may have viewed the

In 1937 and 1938 the 24-foot Gar Wood was the only utility built that featured a runabout-style folding-V windshield. This attractively designed windshield was a major advantage over other builders of utility models. *Classic Boating*

In 1938 Gar Wood upstaged its rivals when it introduced the totally unique rear-engine *Streamliner*. Using Chrysler's new V-drive Crown engine, this 22-footer was styled like a runabout with the room of a utility. *Gar Wood*

Production Volume for 1937

Stock Model	Description	Quantity	Price
Model 700 to 703	16-foot runabout	40 units	$1,385 to $1,805
Model 705 to 709	16-foot Speedster	1 unit	$1,565 to $2,045
Model 710 to 714	18-foot runabout	7 units	$1,725 to $2,475
Model 720 to 724	19-foot runabout	34 units	$1,890 to $2,565
Model 725 to 732	22-foot runabout	12 units	$2,495 to $3,850
Model 735 to 743	25-foot runabout	9 units	$3,375 to $5,275
Model 745 to 753	28-foot runabout	3 units	$5,995 to $7,720
Model 754	28-foot landau	1 unit	$6,770 to $7,000
Model 755 to 762	33-foot runabout	0	$9,170 to $12,800
Model 765 to 767	18-foot utility	19 units	$1,350 to $1,640
Model 770 to 772	18-foot cabin utility	22 units	$1,545 to $1,835
Model 775 to 778	20-foot utility	24 units	$1,585 to $2,175
Model 780 to 784	20-foot cabin utility	63 units	$2,000 to $2,645
Model 786 to 794	24-foot utility	7 units	$3,045 to $5,345
Model 7000 to 7008	24-foot cabin utility	19 units	$3,495 to $5,795
Model 7012 to 7014	26-foot cruiser	3 units	$2,995
Model 7022	32-foot Ex. Cruiser	3 units	$11,900

Total production for 1937: 267 units

boat division with a tougher eye toward the bottom line. The decision to share the boat facility with the bus division was a vivid example of the new attitude from headquarters

The unanticipated decision to sell the bus division removed a serious internal dilemma for the boat division, but not before the permanent loss of boat production for 1938. There was every reason to believe that 1938 would have been a record-setting year for Gar Wood Boat sales. The rivals at Chris-Craft had an outstanding sales year, leaving Gar Wood and its dealers far behind when the 1938 market share was reviewed. The untimely death of Logan Wood in 1938 and the ill-conceived decision to move the bus operations to Marysville deprived the boat division of a vital season of certain success. The company's reduced production hurt Gar Wood dealers who were unable to secure timely delivery dates and lost sales to its competition. The shadow cast by the bus issue impacted sales volume for the next three years.

There were seven 22-foot Streamliners built in 1938. Two of them were sold as 1939 models and

In 1937 Gar Wood introduced the 19-foot Custom runabout to replace the popular 18-foot *Special*. The new runabout provided significantly more passenger room and extensive power options. *Tom Anthony*

Production Volume for 1938

Stock Model	Description	Quantity	Price
Models 800 to 805	16-foot runabout	15 units	$1,385 to $1,950
Models 806 to 809	16-foot Speedster	0	$1,565 to $2,045
Models 810 to 814	19-foot runabout	10 units	$1,890 to $2,365
Models 815 to 824	22-foot runabout	5 units	$2,595 to $3,895
Models 825 to 834	25-foot runabout	4 units	$3,275 to $6,500
Models 835 to 840	28-foot runabout	2 units	$5,995 to $7,220
Model 841 L	28-foot landau	0	$6,770
Model 845	33-foot runabout	0	$9,670
Model 846 L	33-foot landau	0	$12,470
Models 850 to 855	18-foot utility	8 units	$1,350 to $1,945
Models 860 to 865	18-foot Cabin utility	12 units	$1,545 to $2,145
Models 870 to 875	20-foot utility	11 units	$1,585 to $2,180
Models 880 to 884	20-foot cabin utility	24 units	$2,030 to $2,505
Models 890 to 899	24-foot utility	5 units	$3,205 to $5,375
Models 8000 to 8009	24-foot cabin utility	7 units	$3,655 to $5,825
Model 915, 923,123	22-foot Streamliner	7 units	$2,625 to $2,955
Model [Experimental]	[Military Target Boat]	Unknown	33-foot special
Model[Experimental]	[Military Target Boat]	Unknown	20-foot VD

Total production for 1938: 114 units

one was sold two years later as a 1940 model. The first 17 hull numbers recorded as 1938 models were actually built in 1937 and stored over the winter in the factory. These 17 boats were then assigned 1938 model numbers and counted as part of the 1938 production volume.

The first 33-foot Special was produced in 1938 for the Intercontinent Corporation of New York City. It was powered by a 425-horsepower Gar Wood Liberty and was, in reality, the first of the target boats that Wood was promoting to the military for gunnery training. Over the next two years the clandestine Intercontinent Corporation purchased eight more of these 33-foot Specials, giving Gar Wood an early start in providing military craft to the government. Another unusual product for 1938 was hull #6243, listed only as "20-foot VD" and retained by the company until mid-1940. It appears to have been another experimental V-drive craft in the mode of the successful Streamliner concept.

It is interesting to observe that Gar Wood continued to carry its 33-foot runabout and its 16-foot Speedster in its sales brochures and national advertising long after interest in them diminished. The last three Speedsters were built in 1936 and would

not be purchased until 1941. The last 33-foot runabout to be sold, hull #5460, was actually built in 1930 and shipped to Eugenio Silvani in Milan, Italy, in 1934 as a current model with a new hull number. In spite of the lack of interest in both of these models, they remained in Gar Wood sales brochures through 1940.

In 1938 minimum wages in America were increased to 40 cents per hour and the maximum work week was trimmed to 44 hours. Howard Hughes set a new world record flying around the world in less than four days to publicize the forthcoming New York World's Fair. The fair's theme was "Progress and Peace." Before the year was over Germany claimed Austria and the Sudetenland. Orson Wells frightened the country with his realistic radio broadcast of *War of the Worlds*.

The goal for the 1938 models was to continue to improve and make refinements to the very successful Trophy Fleet of 1937. Gar Wood's press release prior to the New York boat show stated, ". . . more beautiful streamlining, with greater freeboard, wider beam, more pronounced flare and numerous refinements in bottom lines which will result in greatly enhanced riding comfort and maneuverability. All models are wider and roomier and visibility in all models has been increased. The sixteen foot runabout, the twenty-two foot runabout, the twenty-five foot runabout and the twenty-eight foot runabout have all been completely redesigned."

The major news for 1938 was the successful development of a totally new 22-foot rear-engine "Streamliner" runabout. This boat once again demonstrated the creative skills of the Gar Wood designers who were leading the field in so many areas. The boat was styled as a runabout with the walk-around room of a utility model. For its length and style it was exceptionally roomy with a very companionable new seating arrangement. It was the first stock runabout to feature a barrel bow and a barrel stern. The patented V-drive configuration meant

Twin six-cylinder Chrysler Crown engines power this 1938 25-foot triple cockpit runabout. Gar Wood had the engineering skill to offer its customers a wide variety of engine options. *Classic Boating*

more speed from the same horsepower and consequently greater cruising range and improved fuel economy. The Streamliner was noticeably quieter due to the engine location and improved principles of engine compartment soundproofing, including a new water-jacketed engine silencer.

The prototype model Streamliner had several innovations, and its refreshing appearance seemed to express the excitement that the boat division was feeling. The first Streamliner sported a canvas-covered deck. Rising up boldly along the centerline of the fore deck was a mahogany fin running the full length of the deck from the bow to the windshield. Rather than the traditional cut water, the Streamliner had a narrow stem band that drew attention to the forward end of the sheer plank that curved back into the top of a rounded stem. This created a unique barreling of the bow. It was a boat loaded with ideas, of which some were incorporated into the company's production models. The new Streamliner was a concept boat that served notice to the boating industry of a new level of creativity at Gar Wood.

If there were any positive results from the misguided intrusion of bus manufacturing into the boat factory, it was the determination by George Joachim to restyle every 1939 model to be so attractive that every potential buyer would be drawn to the advantages of owning a Gar Wood. Each of the five standard Gar Wood runabout models would be given the distinctive barrel bow treatment developed with the Streamliner. Gar Wood's method of creating a barrel bow required a difficult reverse curve in the forward end of the sheer plank and rounding the upper portion of the stem. It took superb craftsmanship to achieve the complete barrel effect. The results were outstanding and Gar Wood accomplished exactly the effect it wanted. The top of the stainless-steel cutwater gave the illusion of being split into flowing wings that blend smartly into the rub rails along the sheer.

The technique used by Gar Wood to achieve the successful curvature of the sheer planks still challenges contemporary woodworkers and boat restoration experts. The Turcotte Brothers, famous for re-creating Gar Wood's best designs, still marvel at the skill required by woodworkers to successfully achieve this type of barrel bow styling on a production line.

The editorial staff of *Rudder* magazine described Gar Wood's 1939 Trophy Fleet this way:

Every model has been completely redesigned in a new ultra-smart streamlined treatment, further accentuating the smooth flowing lines and distinctive styling which has always been characteristic of boats

The 22-foot *Streamliner's* twin gas tanks are located under the side seats in the aft cockpit. This unique, passenger-friendly seating arrangement brought a welcome quality to the runabout style. *Classic Boating*

of Gar Wood manufacture. Larger, roomier, more beautiful boats with more horsepower—newer and more streamlined hulls—still finer finish and more luxurious equipment are offered. Through increased manufacturing efficiency and greatly increased sales volume, prices have been reduced from $25 to $1,970, reductions running as high as 10 percent in some instances.

A new barrel bow, of unusual streamlined design, patterned, it is said, after that of the trans-Atlantic liner, the *Queen Mary*, is a feature of all Gar Wood custom runabouts. The 16-foot Custom Runabout has many features characteristic of the larger Gar Wood runabouts. It has a 5 foot 9 inch beam, exceptional width in a boat of this length, and will carry its five passengers swiftly and smartly. To the instrument panel, unusual for its beautiful indirect translucent lighting, have been added a gas and water temperature gauge. Upholstery is genuine leather, of the same fine grain quality used in all Gar Wood Boats.

In the 22-foot rear-engine Streamliner will be seen one of the most modern boats in the entire boating field, a boat which combines hydroplane action with runabout stability. A patented V-drive hook-up places the engine well aft, permitting unusual seating capacity, in what is believed to be the first triple cockpit boat ever offered. Miles faster with the same power, due to a new bottom and a hull design which takes full advantage of the rear-engine installation, this new Gar Wood combines minimum wetted surface with maximum riding comfort and seaworthiness.

The flagship of the new 1939 Gar Wood runabout fleet is the beautifully streamlined, sumptuously appointed new 28-foot Custom Runabout. This runabout has a double cockpit forward and a single cockpit aft, both equipped with a V-type folding windshield. An ice box is standard equipment. Eleven passengers can be seated comfortably. The engine in the Show boat model is a 12-cylinder 316 horsepower Scripps which will drive the boat up to 46 miles per hour. Four twin-screw motor options are also available.

Of outstanding interest, perhaps, is the new Gar Wood Overniter, one of the unusual boats of the year. Named Overniter because of its comfortable sleeping quarters for two in a roomy trunk cabin under the forward deck, this boat is really a combined commuter and utility, with speeds up to 41 m.p.h. The boat has 8 feet 4 inches beam and a cockpit 11 feet 5 inches long with ample room for two fishing chairs, folding yacht chairs or rear cockpit seat. The cabin has 54-inch headroom and is equipped with two 6 foot 2 inch berths, covered with a coral mohair blend. Other standard features include ice box, storage compartments, toilet, dual electric trumpets, etc. A stove and a collapsible navy top are optional at extra cost. A newly styled, rounded-corner motor box, insulated against noise and heat, houses the marine motor of which a wide selection is offered.

The Overniter was a superb pocket cruiser that was built on the proven hull of Gar Wood's husky 24-foot, 6-inch utility. Capable of great speed and rugged performance this small express cruiser was an ideal craft for commuting, open water fishing, and spending a night aboard. It was one of the surprise hits of the 1939 New York boat show. George Joachim's keen sense of styling transformed the cabin enclosures on the 20-foot, 6-inch and the 24-foot, 6-inch cabin utilities into the most stunning and attractive designs at the show. The Gar Wood display was sensational, and the dealers loved what they saw. Clearly the Gar Wood team had outdone themselves by refining boats that were already considered the finest of their type.

The editorial writers for the boating journals wrote glowing reviews about Gar Wood's Trophy Fleet and praised every model in the line as the best of its type and predicted enthusiastic acceptance from domestic and overseas buyers. In regard to the already popular streamlined cabin utilities, a *Motor Boating* magazine article stated "unquestionably the most handsomely finished and luxuriously equipped boats of their length. Ideal for commuting, cruising and fishing with the speed of the fastest runabouts these attractive sedans are the pinnacle of design achievement.

"The cabin utilities have been completely redesigned to embody the latest principles of streamlining while successfully improved and refined. Glass area in the V-type ventilating windshield has been increased 10 per cent. The window frames and windshield corner posts have been narrowed. This improves visibility and adds materially to riding enjoyment. The coaming has been drawn out back to

Restyled for 1939 the 20-foot, 6-inch Streamline Cabin Utility was a stunning craft that gave elegant dignity to a practical boat. It remains as one of the most attractively styled classics of all time. *Jim Brown*

the rear cockpit seat and the cabin roof curves gracefully into the top of the side coamings trimmed over its full width with leather-covered crash molding."

Chris-Craft's outstanding success from 1938 continued without missing a beat as that company began to dominate the cruiser market. Chris-Craft's rivalry with Gar Wood seemed less important because Chris-Craft's ever-expanding dealer network seemed to order boats as fast as the company could build them. There seemed to be no question that in the realm of runabouts, utilities, and cabin utilities Gar Wood's designs led the industry. It was also true that to purchase a Gar Wood in 1939, a buyer needed to spend significantly more money than for the same model Chris-Craft.

Here is a sample comparison of similar models with similar power at January 1, 1939, listed prices:

Gar Wood's cabin utility models led the industry in style and performance every year. In 1937 the 20-footer, illustrated here, was the year's most popular model with 63 boats sold. *Gar Wood*

Model	Chris-Craft List Price	Gar Wood List Price
16-foot Runabout	$1,390	$1,540
19-foot Runabout	$1,540	$1,980
23-foot Runabout	$1,690	$2,720
27-foot Runabout	$3,050	$5,635
18-foot Utility	$1,195	$1,505
22-foot Utility	$1,495	$1,830
25-foot Utility	$2,650	$3,585

This chart provides comparable data on similar models of Chris-Crafts and Gar Woods. Each of the models selected had similar size engines and comparable speeds. The difference was in the styling, the quality of the appointments, assumptions about performance, and some differences in beam, freeboard, and detailing. The Gar Woods all had leather upholstery. Only the 25-foot Chris-Craft Sportsman Utility had leather upholstery. The Gar Woods were built of furniture-grade African mahogany, while Chris-Craft used Philippine mahogany. In 1939 would a prospective buyer select the 16-foot, 6-inch Gar Wood over the 16-foot Chris-Craft if it cost $150 more, or the 19-foot, 6-inch Gar Wood for $440 more than the 19-foot Chris-Craft? These were the types of choices that buyers had to make, and most buyers never had the opportunity to compare the boats side by side.

To announce its new models properly Gar Wood produced one of its finest catalogs. It was 26 pages

Production Volume for 1939

Stock Model	Description	Quantity	Price
Models 900 to 905	16-foot runabout	13 units	$1,340 to $1,845
Models 910 to 914	19-foot runabout	25 units	$1,700 to $2,125
Models 915 to 921	22-foot runabout	2 units	$2,440 to $3,660
Models 923, 924	22-foot Streamliner	8 units	$2,625 to $2,955
Models 925 to 934	25-foot runabout	0	$3,075 to $6,100
Models 935 to 941	28-foot runabout	3 units	$5,635 to $6,785
Models 945, 946 L	33-foot runabout	0	$9,000 to 10,500
Models 950 to 955	18-foot, 6-inch utility	18 units	$1,295 to $1,810
Models 960 to 965	18-foot, 6-inch cabin utility	18 units	$1,520 to $2,035
Models 970 to 975	20-foot, 6-inch utility	17 units	$1,530 to $2,100
Models 980 to 984	20-foot, 6-inch cabin utility	32 units	$2,000 to $2,420
Models 990 to 999	24-foot, 6-inch utility	5 units	$3,135 to $5,105
Models 9000 to 9009	24-foot, 6-inch cabin utility	11 units	$3,585 to $5,555
Models 9100 to 9114	24-foot, 6-inch Overniter	8 units	$2,995 to $5.410

Total production for 1939: 160 units

It's easy to see why the 1939–1941 20-foot, 6-inch Streamline Cabin Utility is considered to be one of the most attractive and best-performing enclosed models of the golden era.

with a full-color cover and color used effectively throughout the brochure, which featured 64 photographs and the deck plans of every model. This catalog was an important breakthrough for Gar Wood, which had a reputation of being very tight with its advertising budget and was guilty of having graphic artists touch up older photos to make the boats appear to be the new models. Gar Wood's rivals at Chris-Craft took a much different approach and developed the most enticing ads and catalogs in the industry.

In 1939 the unique barrel bow styling developed on the first Streamliner would become the standard treatment on all Gar Wood runaout models. *Classic Boating*

Gar Wood also prepared a large, full-color poster illustrating a romantic scene of a couple snuggled close together in a custom runabout heading out slowly for an evening cruise. The caption read, "Half the enjoyment is knowing it's a Gar Wood." This poster was a promotional masterpiece and one of the rarest of all Gar Wood memorabilia items.

Gar Wood's sales for 1939 showed a 40 percent increase over the sales volume of 1938. It fell short of the company's expectations due to lost time changing over the factory from the modifications for fabricating buses and the effect of lost market share in 1938.

It was a year of extremes. Pan Am's new sea plane, the *Yankee Clipper*, began scheduled flights to Europe. America was host to a spectacular World's Fair in Flushing Meadows, New York. A magnificent Perisphere and Trylon symbolized the event with the theme of Progress and Peace. *Gone with the Wind* and the *Wizard of Oz* turned out to be the year's most memorable films. By year's end Germany invaded Poland. Britain and France declared war on Germany, and the stage was set for world conflict on a scale that exceeded our worst fears.

The concern over war in Europe began eroding Gar Wood's overseas market from its peak years in the mid-1930s to just four boats shipped to customers in Egypt, Sweden, Belgium, and Switzerland in 1939. Gar Wood's international reputation for setting world speed records had led to dealers and customers in two dozen nations. But with the increasing

Instrument Panels

Correct instrument panels and gauges are vital to maintaining the authenticity and character of classic boats. Throughout its production years, Gar Wood was rather conservative with instrumentation and changes were infrequent. In the brief postwar period, at least four different dashboard instrument panel styles were used. The designs were selected based largely on the availability due to constant equipment and supply shortages. The following photographs provide an interesting sample of Gar Wood's various instrument panel designs and the gauges most frequently used.

A 1947 16-foot Ensign utility.

A 1936 25-foot twin engine Custom runabout.

A 1930 28-foot limousine.

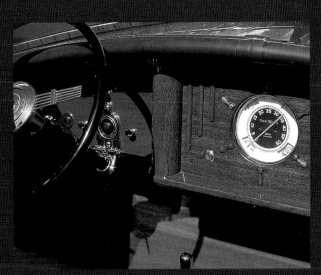

The 1938 22-foot Custom runabout.

The 28-foot *Flagship* runabout offered the beautiful and powerful 316-horsepower Scripps V-12 engine. It is one of the most expensive of all marine engines. *Classic Boating*

likelihood of global war, opportunities for foreign sales disappeared.

In 1939 Wood's former partner and rival, Chris Smith, died at age 74. Their partnership from 1916 to 1922 formed the greatest team in the history of speedboat racing. Wood continued to triumph in the field for 11 more years after their breakup, before his competition virtually gave up. Smith's family went on to become one of the world's most successful boatbuilders. The split in 1922 never ended their friendship or their respect for each other. Their boatbuilding rivalry was similar to two determined champions going at each other for all they were worth to see whose boats were best. When the dust cleared, the winners were, and are, the thousands of Chris-Craft and Gar Wood owners who enjoy the superb boats that were improved by their competition.

Chris Smith turned over control of the boat business to his son Jay in late 1924 and by 1927 officially made him president. It was Jay who persuaded his father to break with Wood in 1922. Jay and his brother Bernard were more aggressive than their father in the competition with Gar Wood Boats. In spite of their great success and their vast dealer network, the Smiths were always sensitive about Gar Wood's image as the premier boatbuilder. When Jay declared that Chris-Craft was the world's largest builder of motorboats, Gar Wood immediately announced that it was "the largest exclusive manufacturer of runabouts and utilities in the world"

Production Volume for 1940

Stock Model	Description	Quantity	Price
Models 100 to 105	16-foot runabout	6 units	$1,415 to $2,020
Models 110 to 114	19-foot runabout	26 units	$1,790 to $2,315
Models 115 to 121	22-foot runabout	3 units	$2,640 to $4,095
Models 123, 124	22-foot Streamliner	2 units	$2,795 to $3,455
Models 125 to 134	25-foot runabout	1 unit	$3,395 to $6,800
Models 135 to 141	28-foot runabout	2 units	$5,535 to $6,335
Models 143, 144	33-foot runabout	0	$9,900 to $11,400
Models 145 to 147	18-foot, 6-inch utility	9 units	$1,095 to $1,295
Models 150 to 155	18-foot, 6-inch utility	20 units	$1,420 to $1,985
Models 160 to 165	18-foot, 6-inch cabin utility	13 units	$1,696 to $2,260
Models 170 to 175	20-foot, 6-inch utility	19 units	$1,655 to $2,275
Models 180 to 184	20-foot, 6-inch cabin utility	39 units	$2,475 to $2,645
Models 190 to 199	24-foot, 6-inch utility	4 units	$3,640 to $5,130
Models 1000 to 1009	24-foot, 6-inch cabin utility	7 units	$3,640 to $5,580
Models 1100 to 1115	24-foot, 6-inch Overniter	11 units	$2,995 to $5,410
Model 1142	30-foot Commuter	1 unit	$8,225
Models 1154, 1158	30-foot Commodore	2 units	$8,005 to $9,195

Total production for 1940: 165 units

and carried that statement in ads and brochures.

The death of Logan Wood in 1938 and Chris Smith just a year later hurried Wood's decision to spend even more time traveling, flying, and doing the things he enjoyed best. When it was obvious that there were no eager challengers for his Harmsworth Trophy, he officially announced his retirement from racing. Flying had replaced racing in his life and he traveled extensively around the country in his own planes. He also wanted to devote more time to his inventions and military applications of small craft that could be used effectively in the war he was sure was close at hand.

Ed Hancock and Jack Clifford decided to make the 1940 New York Boat Show a grand showcase of their outstanding Trophy Fleet. They displayed 11 models, the largest array of Gar Wood Boats ever brought to this show. The list of display boats included the 16- and 19-foot custom runabouts; the 22-foot Streamliner; the 28-foot custom runabout with the 12-cylinder Scripps; the 18-foot, 6-inch open utility with a four-cylinder Gray (their lowest-priced boat); the 18-foot, 6-inch cabin utility; the 20-foot, 6-inch custom utility; the 20-foot, 6-inch and the 24-foot, 6-inch streamline cabin utilities; the 24-foot, 6-inch Overniter; and their headliner, the 24-foot, 6-inch custom open utility with a gleaming white hull and twin Chrysler Crown engines. Each model was carefully selected and built in the fall for the show.

The handsome and practical cabin utilities made up 40 percent of the 1940 production and when combined with open utilities and pocket cruisers they accounted for 75 percent of Gar Wood's 1940 production. There was a strong movement toward boats offering more flexibility, room, and shelter than the sporty runabouts.

Once again George Joachim and his design team came up with a superb, high-performance 30-foot cruiser hull, which gave them two new models for 1941. One version of the new 30-foot hull was a model called the Commuter, a stunning design that could exceed 40 miles per hour in a perfect planning attitude. This boat was absolutely unique. There was no other craft like it. The U.S. Border Patrol used a special version of it to guard the national waterfront. As an all-weather water taxi,

The 24-foot, 6-inch custom utility was totally restyled for 1940. It was featured at the New York boat show with twin Chrysler Crowns and drew rave reviews from the marine reporters covering the event.

pilot boat, patrol craft, or rescue vessel its design was straightforward and attractive.

The alternate version was the Commodore, which was the next step up from the sporty Overniter. Just like the Overniter, it had blazing speed. The larger size provided more interior space with a full galley and sleeping accommodations for four adults. It could be a rugged and safe fishing boat and was fast enough for water-skiing.

In addition to the new 30-foot models for 1941, Joachim came up with new styling ideas for all of the existing models in the line. All of the runabouts would have barrel sterns, and the transoms would be raked aft, adding 6 inches to their length. On the runabouts the top of the transom would be rounded into the aft deck giving a smooth flow from the deck to the transom. It would require a great deal of hand shaping to achieve the desired effect. Joachim had a remarkable flare for creative styling that was always in good taste and in keeping with the Gar Wood tradition. Of equal importance was his knowledge of woodworking techniques that provided practical methods to incorporate attractive innovations into production lines. He also decided to include the barrel bow styling on the 24-foot, 6-inch hull, thus providing three additional models— the open utility, the cabin utility, and the Overniter— with this feature. The Overniter was completely restyled and transformed into the most attractive small express cruiser in the industry. It now sported a distinctive three-section mahogany-trimmed windshield, a military visor style cabin roof, sporty white canvas spray panels, and a unique removable hardtop.

The 1941 sales literature followed the red-white-and-blue patriotic theme that was beginning to sweep the nation. The new Gar Wood catalog was large and

continued on page 100

Special Gar Wood features

One of the many interesting characteristics of Gar Wood Boats was the special attention paid to detailing and attractive features. These features are usually treasured by the boat owners but often overlooked by casual observers. In this section we have created several photographs to share some of these examples of Gar Wood's special features.

The boats feature lavish use of bright deck trim.

The aft cockpit windshields fold down on the larger runabouts.

The split cutwaters and flared boot stripes are on the post–World War II models.

The stylish bow treatment is featured on all the runabouts.

The larger runabouts used combination windshield bracket and light.

This is a built-in icebox on larger runabouts and utilities.

This boat features built-in lockers for larger utilities.

Even the step pads received special attention.

Limousines featured a crystal bud vase.

Racing-style gas caps for quick fill-ups.

Continued from page 97

impressive with color images of each model. An interesting spin-off from the company's new catalog was a set of individual brochure sheets, printed on both sides in color, describing each model. The images came directly from the deluxe catalog and allowed the dealers to give customers a single-page flyer on the model that interested them rather than the complete and somewhat costly catalog. To capitalize on the extraordinary new styling, Gar Wood's advertising theme for 1941 was, "Streamlined Fun For '41."

The editorial writers for *Motor Boating* magazine gave the new models glowing reviews after their first viewing.

Gar Wood launches the 1941 season with the most comprehensive and ambitious boat building program in the company's history. It offers a smartly-styled, new Trophy Fleet comprising sixteen different series of open and enclosed boats, which includes thirty-six deluxe and custom runabouts, sixty-one utility types, and twenty-eight 30-foot boats. This variety and number establish Gar Wood as one of the largest individual boat builders in the world of these sizes and types.

For 1941, Gar Wood's naval architects and boat builders have incorporated greater seaworthiness, more speed, luxury, comfort and eye-appealing beauty, more refinements and appointments than any other line previously presented. The new 1941 styles represent decided advancement in design and engineering achievement. The new boats are softer and drier riding. Crown surfaces replace flat ones; straight lines and sharp angles are eliminated; deck sections are gracefully crowned. The decidedly increased flare forward, in addition to providing drier rides, establishes a smart new contour for Gar Wood creations. New type military visors, barrel bows, barrel sterns, blue-colored non-rumble tops, new type windshields with increased visibility and safety glass all around are some of the numerous 1941 innovations. The models have distinguishing names such as: Flagship, Comet, Skipper, Vacationer, Royale, Aristocrat, American, Overniter, Commuter and Commodore.

All cabin roofs are painted blue; bottoms are red, boot tops white, carrying out the new national color scheme of red, white and blue. Replacing the so-called one man top is the new Landau top available on the 24'-6" utility and the 22'-6" Streamliner providing protection with an abundance of fresh air and openness.

All models are custom built by craftsmen steeped in the tradition of upholding the high quality standard of boats bearing that world famous name—*Gar Wood*.

By this time the company was very skilled at placing favorable press in the most widely read boating publications. Gar Wood Boats were of

Leading Lady, Gar Wood's 1940 New York show model with twin engines, demonstrates how this husky 24-foot, 6-inch utility provides runabout performance at high speed. *Classic Boating*

unsurpassed quality and style, and their popularity was good for the sport and the publications devoted to it. Lengthy praise by boating writers and editors was valuable publicity that money couldn't buy.

For the 1941 line, cabin roofs were extended slightly over the windshields, creating the military visor look that was smart and practical. Never before had so many design innovations been incorporated in one model year. Even more remarkable was that the improvements were made on designs that were considered on the leading edge of crisp styling already. The new models were recognized by members of the marine industry for outstanding design achievement and superb craftsmanship. It seemed inconceivable that anymore could have been done to improve on the 1941 Trophy Fleet.

What no one knew at the time was that this beautiful fleet of boats that had evolved gradually over 20 years at the hands of a few dedicated craftsmen would be the end of the line of this generation of Gar Wood Boats. In less than 12 months military obligations and government defense contracts would interrupt production of the 1941 Trophy Fleet for the duration of World War II. Customers, dealers, and the workers themselves all anticipated that when the war ended, the wonderful Gar Wood designs of 1941 would be the logical

starting point for postwar production. Of course it was logical, but the next four years brought many changes to the company. In 1941, before the declaration of war, Gar Wood announced his retirement from Gar Wood Industries, leaving the boat factory to fend for itself in the postwar corporate power struggle. George Joachim died in 1943 while supervising Gar Wood's military production in Marysville. Nap Lisee left when work at the Algonac plant gradually diminished and was working in Sarnia, Ontario, for the Canadian shipbuilding firm known as Mac-Craft, supervising the construction of 112-foot sub chasers.

Gar Wood's new sales brochures printed in the fall adapted the dual theme of "The Boat For You In '42" along with "Quality Pays These Defense Days." Gar Wood had seven boats that were officially designated as 1942 models—three 19-foot, 6-inch runabouts; two 18-foot, 6-inch cabin utilities (one Overniter and one Commuter); and two 20-foot, 6-inch cabin utilities (again, an Overniter and a Commuter). They were all built in 1941 and would have been used in the 1942 boat show if there had been one. The December 7, 1941, the attack on Pearl Harbor by the Japanese ended pleasure craft production at Gar Wood and drew the United States into World War II.

Production Volume for 1941

Stock Model	Description	Quantity	Price
Models 1 to 6	16-foot, 6-inch Deluxe Runabout	11 units	$1,850 to $2,490
Models 10 to 14	19-foot, 6-inch Deluxe Runabout	27 units	$2,265 to $2,820
Models 15 to 21	22-foot, 6-inch Deluxe Runabout	2 units	$3,235 to $4,470
Model 23	22-foot, 6-inch Streamliner	3 units	$3,470
Model 24	22-foot, 6-inch Landau Streamliner	1 unit	$3,770
Models 25 to 34	25-foot, 6-inch Custom Runabout	2 units	$4,140 to $7,55
Models 35 to 40	28-foot, 6-inch Custom Runabout	0	$7,060 to $8,845
Models 45 to 47	18-foot, 6-inch Utility	1 unit	$1,495 to $1,690
Models 50 to 55	18-foot, 6-inch Utility	16 units	$1,855 to $2,470
Models 60 to 65	18-foot, 6-inch Cabin Utility	10 units	$2,155 to $2,770
Models 70 to 75	20-foot, 6-inch Utility	19 units	$2,125 to $2,740
Models 80 to 84	20-foot, 6-inch Cabin Utility	17 units	$2,710 to $3,240
Models 90 to 99	24-foot, 6-inch Utility	6 units	$3,850 to $5,635
Models 100 to 109	24-foot, 6-inch Cabin Utility	7 units	$4,350 to $6,135
Models 110 to 124	24-foot, 6-inch Overniter	10 units	$3,935 to $6,000
Models 130 to 142	30-foot Commuter	4 units	$7,460 to $11,110
Models 145 to 158	30-foot Commodore	3 units	$8,010 to $11,760
Model Special	33-foot, 6-inch Target Boat	8 units	Unknown

Total production for 1941: 147 units

Military Boat Production

1942 to 1945

Gar Wood's decision to retire in 1941 resulted in new management and the beginning of sweeping changes at Gar Wood Industries. Until 1939 this giant corporation was virtually a one-man company with Wood owning 780,000 of the 800,000 shares of common stock. In that year he sold 320,000 shares of his stock. In 1938, Logan Wood died. Logan's death deeply affected the direction and the future of Gar Wood

The 24-foot Plane Personnel Boat was the Navy's equivalent of the peacetime utility boat. The protective fender material all along the rail anticipates rough service ahead. *Gar Wood*

Industries. For three decades Logan ran the business brilliantly for his brother. He was the one person who made it possible for Gar to pursue all the things in life he enjoyed so much. Gar never had to be concerned with the day-to-day operation of the industry that provided the means for the good life. Logan was the hard driver that this type of industry needed to succeed. He even trained his salesmen and his executives in the shops. Whenever he thought of sales, he thought of service. Salesmen had to be able to stand up to road builders' conventions, and they had to slide under dump trucks if necessary. Logan and the company always considered the customer as sacrosanct as the government considers the Constitution. Logan was always fair, but he expected his staff to go anywhere and do anything that kept their customers loyal to their products. Gar knew how valuable Logan and his brothers had been to this industry and to him personally. With Logan gone, Gar faced the choice of picking up the reins his brother had effectively held, or divesting himself of control. With such a good life to enjoy, but diminishing years to do so, Gar chose the latter.

Other companies paid their men much more than Gar Wood Industries paid its employees. Gar Wood's technique of keeping this good staff together was never quite clear, though several explanations were speculated: Logan Wood inspired loyalty; Glen Bassett, treasurer, was expert at controlling factions and promoting camaraderie; employees liked to work for a famous champion racer who could call them by their first names when he dropped in. One executive speculated, "Maybe some of us thought that someday Gar would step out and there would be a melon to cut."

Glen Bassett was the logical choice to replace Logan Wood as corporate president and could provide the necessary leadership in an uneasy period when American involvement in the war seemed inevitable. Wood sold the balance of his common stock in early 1941, dispersing ownership so completely that no one stockholder had as much as one-half of 1 percent of the total. This sale was preceded by a maneuver to spread over a number of years the cost of buying out Wood's control: Part of the par value of his holdings was converted into nonvoting preferred stock. A New York banking syndicate handled the common stock that was put on public sale and helped disentangle Wood's personal and corporate affairs. Wood bought his Detroit mansion, Grayhaven, for $100,000. He also became chairman of the board at $25,000 a year. In 1943 his preferred stock was retired, and in 1945 he resigned as chairman of the board. He was replaced by New York investment banker, John Bergen, who brought two other bankers to the board.

The new officers of the company were all veteran company men. Glen Bassett, former treasurer and company troubleshooter, was made president. Ralph Jenkins, who had worked his way up from the shop, was named vice president and general manager, handling the complex job of production and supervising sales.

In time these changes in leadership impacted heavily on the boat division's future. Both Gar and Logan had always been there to ward off any criticism on the boat division's modest sales volume and lack of profitability. Many corporate executives felt their salaries might have been significantly higher if the boat division had been forced to operate profitably. It was certain that the new executives would keep a wary eye on boat production and profit.

Early in 1941 Gar Wood offered the government full access to the boat factory for construction of military craft if necessary. With America's declaration of war in December 1941, production of pleasure craft was immediately discontinued at Marysville

The 33-foot radio-controlled Target Boat was a special Gar Wood concept, which the Army found to be vital for training gunnery personnel on rapidly moving targets. *Gar Wood*

The 36-foot, 6-inch Navy Picket Boat was built by several marine contractors. Documented testimony indicates that Navy personnel considered the Gar Wood version their favorite. *Gar Wood*

and preparations for military production began. The seven "1942" models were shipped to seven Gar Wood dealers, and the factory was officially ready for its military assignments.

Wood had anticipated the potential use of small craft for military purposes long before 1941. In 1933 Wood discussed moving targets with Army officers and learned that what the Army needed and wanted was a swiftly moving target. The Coast Artillery used tugs, and expensive tugs at that, to tow its targets, and the gunners were often hampered in target practice by the towing vessel.

During practice, seacoast guns are aimed at a target that represents a designated part of an enemy vessel. Success is judged by the fall of shots in relation to the point designated. Previously it had been suggested that speedboats be used as targets, but the Army did not think it was possible to hold a small boat on course without an operator aboard.

Wood listened to their concerns and told them that he believed he could solve their problem. Colonel Sunderland, who was in charge of experimental ordnance at Fortress Monroe, Virginia, encouraged Wood to give it some thought and to let him know as soon as he had something. In the fall of 1933, Wood developed a crude experimental model and held some tests. The tests were encouraging and Wood notified Sunderland of his progress. A complete demonstration was scheduled for the following spring. If it was successful, the Army would purchase the craft for additional testing.

The *Detroit News* covered the test and reported the story this way:

Gar Wood has developed a high speed, pilotless target boat for long range coast defense gunnery practice.

The Government has purchased the first one produced and it will be shipped next week from Marysville, Michigan, to Fortress Monroe, Virginia, Wood said, after demonstrating the target boat in the channel off his experimental shop in Algonac where he designs and builds the Miss America race boats.

If the target proves successful, long range gunnery practice will be revolutionized. Instead of gunners firing from calculations at an object being towed by a tug moving three to five miles per hour, they will be required to gauge a target rushing over the water at a speed from 35 to 40 miles an hour—approximating the speed of torpedo boats and destroyers.

Capt. H.C. Mabbott, a War Department gunnery expert, watched the pilotless target in a test on Lake St. Clair. Following that demonstration the purchase by the Government was approved.

The target consists of a six by eight foot red flag flying from the top of a 25-foot metal mast fastened inboard amidships of a 28-foot open cockpit runabout hull. But it is neither the flag nor the hull nor the 225 horsepower motor that interests the War Department.

The secret of the target's appeal to the gunnery experts lies in a gyroscopic control which is so inexpensive as to make the craft feasible for coast artillery target purposes in the event the boat is struck by a shell and sunk.

The gyroscope, installed in the aft cockpit, controls air pressure power that holds the target boat on a fixed course. The air pressure first comes through a metal and then a rubber tube. A six-pound wheel in the gyroscope turns 10,000 revolutions per minute to suck the air through the tube and into a little two-piston motor.

To this "air" motor—for an "air" motor is what it might be called—is attached the control leading to the craft's rudder. When the boat's course is set, which is done by an adjustment of the gyroscope, the operation of the pistons in the "air" motor hold the helm so true that neither high seas nor deep troughs will change the boat's course.

During the demonstration test the strange looking craft maintained a speed of 40 miles an hour in rough seas and stayed on course without a single problem of any type. The Army was satisfied and presented Wood with the order.

The Army continued to purchase Gar Wood–built target boats over the next six years, and Wood often consulted with other branches of the military on special projects. He worked with Howard Hughes and Henry Kaiser on the huge flying boat that became known as the *Spruce Goose*. The twin-hull Venturi began as a government-sponsored Wood project for the Navy as a prototype aircraft carrier design.

Gar Wood Industries was already a government supplier and was familiar with the complications and requirements of fulfilling government contracts. The boat division received contracts to build vessels for the Navy and Army. This meant steady employment to the boatbuilding crews all year for the duration of the war, which was certainly good news; however, it also meant building heavy-duty military craft of government specification and design. The changeover would require considerable adjustment for Gar Wood craftsmen, who were accustomed to using the finest grade mahogany to build masterpiece-quality boats finished with several hand-rubbed coats of varnish to bring attention to their precise joiner work.

In a matter of weeks the company's modern facilities were transformed into a commercial boat plant to turn out heavy-duty work boats that would experience the worst kind of treatment imaginable. These fine Gar Wood craftsmen were given new assignments to build picket boats, target boats, and 46-foot tow boats out of yellow pine and plywood, and to paint everything battleship gray. The beautiful boats of the 1941 Trophy Fleet would soon be just a

The interior of the Marysville factory in full military production. This illustration shows 25 Plane Personnel Boats in four lines at various stages of completion. *Gar Wood*

fond memory to these expert woodworkers. There was a war to be won, and everyone had a job to do. The situation was similar next door at Chris-Craft, which had contracts to build 1,000 landing craft in the first 12 months of the war.

Government work brought many changes to the riverfront boat factory. The sheer volume of production expected by the government was staggering. Many experienced workers were taken in the military draft. Replacing them and recruiting additional new employees was difficult and required much on-the-job training. Security guards and fences were required all around the Marysville plant, and every employee was required to wear a photo identification badge to enter the facilities. George Joachim and Chris-Craft's Bill MacKerer would meet to share methods to improve production efficiency in fulfillment of their respective government contracts.

The first military craft completed at the Marysville plant was for the Army. It was designated JR-1, a 33-foot, 6-inch Target Boat powered by a 12-cylinder, 500-horsepower Kermath that was shipped by rail car from Marysville on March 16, 1942. Eighteen more Target Boats were built over the next seven months to complete the Army contract. The balance of the work was devoted to contracts with the Navy that called for 24-foot plane personnel boats, 36-foot, 6-inch picket boats, and 46-foot tow boats.

The military contracts kept Gar Wood's production staff fully employed for nearly three years. For many, it was a welcome change from the seasonal work schedule that they had experienced over the years. In the spring of 1943 George Joachim's weak heart finally gave out and he died at 70. With his

The largest military craft built by Gar Wood during the World War II was the 46-foot Tow Boat. Twenty-three of these were completed at the Marysville factory. *Gar Wood*

Government Contract Military Craft Production 1942 to 1944

Model	Quantity
33-foot, 6-inch Target, single, 12-cylinder Kermath, 500 horsepower	19 units
36-foot, 6-inch Picket, pair of Chrysler Royals, 8 cylinders, 145 horsepower each	75 units
24-foot Plane Personnel, single Chrysler Crown, 6 cylinders, 115 horsepower, 1.95:1 R.G.*	71 units
46-foot Wooden Tow Boat, single Chrysler Royal, 8 cylinders, 145 horsepower, 4.48:1 R.G.*	10 units
46-foot Wooden Tow Boat, single Buda Diesel, 150 horsepower	13 units

* R.G. = reduction gear

Total military volume: 188 units

The Marysville factory decorated for the Army-Navy Production Award ceremony to be celebrated on March 17, 1945.

death, Gar Wood Boats lost the man most responsible for its stunning boat designs. His son, Walter, who had worked for years with his father, took over as plant superintendent and kept military production on schedule.

The 33-foot, 6-inch Target Boats were fast, husky craft that could be operated with or without a pilot at high speed. They were designed with substantial flotation tanks to prevent accidental sinking from stray gunfire by practicing gunnery personnel. Powered by 500-horsepower Kermath engines these Tow Boats towed targets and could be operated by remote control for target practice at sustained speeds in excess of 45 miles per hour. These Target Boats were not the same hull configuration as the 33-foot Gar Wood stock runabouts. The military version had much greater beam and was more fully decked over except for a small forward cockpit with a wood-framed windshield of similar design to the 1939–1940 model 24-foot, 6-inch utility. Gar Wood supplied the Army with 19 Target Boats from March 16, 1942, until October 13, 1942. Prior to December 7, 1941, Gar Wood sold nine Target Boats (33-foot Specials) to the Army through the Intercontinent Corporation, a total of 28 units in this group.

The 24-foot Plane Personnel Boat was the military equivalent of the Navy utility boat. It was designed to move 8 to 12 passengers quickly to offshore locations or between ships at anchor. The steering wheel was located in the center of the forward cockpit just behind an unusual folding wood-frame windshield. Its standard Chrysler Crown engine was located amidship under two access hatches. The arrangement provided room for a very large aft cockpit with bench seating all around. The entire aft seating area was protected by a large folding canvas top with access from the aft opening. The wide hull carried its full beam to the transom. The entire shear rail of the boat was equipped with a continuous canvas-covered fender running the full length for heavy-duty protection. This type of craft was often used to transport flight personnel between vessels, to shore locations, or from shore to anchored vessels. These "work horse" boats were indispensable to the Navy and experienced the roughest type of abuse constantly. Chrysler power and Gar Wood construction earned them the reputation for dependable service with the Navy.

The 36-foot, 6-inch Picket Boat was a standardized Navy design built by a variety of boatyards. Gar Wood's contract called for 71 Picket Boats built from May 16, 1942, until January 10, 1943. This craft was an all-purpose boat with excellent speed (25 miles per hour) and superior maneuverability for a vessel its size.

The 46-foot Wooden Tow Boat was a heavy work boat intended to tow larger craft when that type of work was required. The first 10 built were powered with a Chrysler Royal with a 4.48 to 1 reduction drive. The final 13 were powered with a Buda Diesel. Gar Wood's contract for 30 46-foot Wooden Tow Boats was terminated on March 6, 1944, with seven boats still under construction. The Allies now controlled the war, and the government began to reduce its industrial contracts on products that were no longer in critical demand. Gar Wood still had several government contracts, but boat production was no longer essential to final victory.

The final 46-foot Tow Boat in fulfillment of the Army contract is prepared for railroad delivery. The helm enclosure is removed for transportation purposes. *Gar Wood*

Although boat construction dominated the factory, Gar Wood's boat division produced a wide variety of products for the military. Gar Wood Liberty marine engines were sold to allied nations for numerous military applications. Most of this engine work was carried on in the Algonac plant. By the time the war ended, nearly all of the surplus World War I Liberty engines in Gar Wood's possession were put to good use during World War II.

Gar Wood had fulfilled their boat contracts on schedule, or ahead of schedule, for every one of the 188 boats produced since the onset of the war. It was a superb record for a small firm that was used to building small varnished runabouts. The 46-foot military tow boats represented a major challenge to any boatbuilding factory and were handled with unusual resourcefulness by the employees of Gar Wood. On February 17, 1945, Undersecretary of War Robert Patterson bestowed upon "the men and women of the boat division of Gar Wood Industries" the Army-Navy Production Award. This is the highest award for industrial excellence that workers on the home front can receive. The letter went on to state, "This award is your nation's tribute to your patriotism and to your great work in backing up our soldiers on the fighting fronts. The award consists of a flag to be flown above your plant and a lapel pin which every man and woman in your plant may wear as a symbol of high contributions to American freedom."

Thirty-one employees of the boat division served the military in various branches during World War II. Three of these employees had completed their tour of military duty and returned to the factory when the award ceremony took place in 1945.

The formal ceremony was held on March 17, 1945, at the Marysville plant. The 53-piece Marysville High School Band provided music for the ceremony that would include dignitaries from the military and Glen Bassett, president of Gar Wood Industries. Jack Clifford was master of ceremonies, and one of the special features was a rare address by Gar Wood in his final appearance as chairman of the board. Ed Hancock, general manager of the boat division, accepted the flag on behalf of the company and the employees. After the ceremony employees and their families and members of the Marysville High School Band were guests of the management of the boat division at an elaborate buffet supper in the plant. The event was a proud moment for Marysville, especially for everyone connected with this special boat factory.

As the war drew to a close, preparations were under way in anticipation of peacetime boat production. Early forecasts predicted a strong postwar market for automobiles, homes, and boats. Boating magazines painted an exciting picture of attractive and modernistic postwar boats that would be the rage in the postwar boom. Enthusiasts speculated about the new postwar designs. Would Gar Wood start up with the same superb "Trophy Fleet" models right where the company left off in 1941, or would it present entirely new designs? The wondering would soon end.

Postwar Production Boats

1946 and 1947

The last Gar Wood 46-foot Tow Boat built for the Navy was shipped on March 6, 1944, nearly a year and a half before the Japanese officially surrendered on September 2, 1945. There were seven 46-foot Tow Boats in various stages of construction in the Marysville factory when the contract was terminated. The building of military boats for the government was now over for Gar Wood, as the government terminated contracts for

With its exceptional performance and attractive design, the 18-foot, 6-inch utility was an appealing model that enticed customers away from Chris-Craft's 18-foot Sportsman.
Mystic Seaport, Rosenfeld Collection, Mystic, Connecticut

In early 1944, design engineer Ed Kaunitz takes the wheel of the prototype of the 15-foot, 6-inch experimental postwar utility. *Gar Wood*

all craft no longer essential to the war effort. For Gar Wood the termination notice came rather early. Some other boatbuilders, such as Elco, Huckins, and Higgins, continued to produce PT boats for the military right to the end of the war.

Gar Wood's boat division still had defense contracts for other essential products, such as large fiberglass radar housings and winch drums for the Navy. Fully half of the factory had been converted to a machine shop to fabricate winch drums. By terminating its Navy boat construction, however, the company created some space for the development of new boat models for the postwar market. With the early termination of their boat contracts, Gar Wood's designers had abundant time to create a new fleet. This extra time was all that was needed to allow Gar Wood to leap ahead of its competitors with new styling and new models. If the company had been fully involved in defense contracts through the end of the war, Gar Wood's postwar fleet may have involved only restyled versions of its 1941 designs. Major rival Chris-Craft decided to forgo total redesign and get a jump on production with only limited restyling.

As far back as 1943, while fully occupied with constructing military craft for the Navy, Gar Wood's design staff managed to squeeze in time to lay out possible new ideas for postwar pleasure boats. The initial drawings began as a type of morale booster for the men working in the factory during the darker days of the war. The designers would display their futuristic design work on the factory bulletin boards to rekindle thoughts of peacetime production. The

Gar Wood Boatbuilders looked forward to the return of the times when they applied their talent to create the most beautiful speedboats in the world.

Jack Clifford had maintained meaningful contact with all his dealers during the war years. He established creative new programs to recruit new dealers. Clifford knew that he had to expand the dealer organization significantly to meet new production goals. He was concerned about new competition from boatbuilders who declared their intentions to enter the peacetime boat trade. Higgins Industries of New Orleans, builder of PT boats and landing barges, announced its plans two years before the end of the war to enter the pleasure boat market. In filling its government contracts, Higgins built more than 20,000 craft of all types for the government. The company had the resources to be a major competitor for dealers and to lure potential customers. Higgins planned to call the fleet PT Juniors, capitalizing on the success of the company's wartime experience. A "new kind of high-speed hull form covered by a U.S. patent" was developed. Clifford knew that he had to establish his dealers quickly to counter a multitude of new rivals. He wanted new models that would be the most attractive in the industry.

At the time the boat division needed to strike out boldly in a competitive postwar marketplace, profound changes during the prior three years hit home. Joachim, the man most responsible for the design and styling of the distinguished tradition of Gar Wood Boats, died in early 1943. His enormous and invaluable contributions to every phase of production, labor relations, and quality control were lost. Nap Lisee, who designed all the soft riding, planing bottoms retired. And Gar Wood, the man who created Gar Wood Industries and personally watched over the development of the boat division through difficult times, announced his resignation as chairman of the board. The real impact of these critical changes was not felt by the boat division because of the activities connected with secure military contracts. Now, the Gar Wood Boat division was about to enter the uncertain postwar market with few allies at headquarters in Detroit. It was the least productive division in a giant industry that, at best, was indifferent to its traditions as an outstanding boatbuilder. The boat division moved into this new era without three of its most important champions.

Wood's resignation as chairman of the board in 1945 brought immediate organizational changes. One of the first moves of the new board was to overhaul management salaries. When Gar Wood was taking most of the profits, the top salary (except for Logan Wood, who got $40,000) was $12,000 a year, and few executives reached $10,000. Now, the new president, Glen Bassett, and new vice president, Ralph Jenkins, would each be paid $47,500. Treasurer Edward Boehm would receive $32,500. The new board included New York City bankers who learned more about winches, hoists, furnaces, and boats. The board held meetings in New York where management learned about vintage wines and the Stork Club. One result of the amalgamation of interests was the hiring of the noted industrial designer Norman Bel Geddes. The goal was to restyle the company's whole line, from boats to bulldozers, under the belief that handsome dump trucks would sell better than ugly ones. Another result was the hiring of Benjamin Sonnenberg, New York public relations specialist, to reform the corporate image.

The war years had been good for Gar Wood Industries. The key reason was that nearly the entire product line could supply the government defense effort without significant alterations to its normal civilian production. The company never really converted its product line when it got into war work; it simply expanded. Before the war Gar Wood Industries produced hoists, truck bodies, road machinery, winches, cranes, truck tanks, and furnaces. From 1941 to 1945 these peacetime products accounted for $145 million of the company's $155 million volume

during the war years. And at war's end only a few days were required to make the changes for supplying civilian, rather than military, customers.

In the summer of 1943 Boehm went to a termination forum at New York University. His experience at the forum was extremely beneficial, and he returned full of valuable ideas. In April 1944, he set up a contract termination department, which had 18 trained employees ready and waiting for the end of their defense contracts. The contract termination department didn't cost Gar Wood a penny, since the expense of closing down government contracts was part of the termination claim. Even before the war ended, the department entered into signed agreements with the Detroit Ordinance District on accounting procedures and profit ratios. This done, it was only a matter of applying a formula to effect a settlement. When the contracts were terminated, Gar Wood had its money in exactly 88 days.

For Gar Wood Industries wartime contracts increased its total production by four times. From 1936 through 1940, Gar Wood's average sales volume was $9,330,000; from 1941 through 1944, it was $38,400,000. Since Gar Wood Industries made virtually the same products in war as in peace, it didn't face expensive retooling costs to return to civilian production. The transition process at the Ford Motor Company, for example, from building B-24 Liberator Bombers to manufacturing automobiles, was a monumental task after the war ended. Gar Wood's challenge was to keep volume high enough to meet its new production capacity. Management's goal would be satisfied if it could maintain $15 to $25 million annually, about half of the annual wartime volume level.

With the new board of trustees reflecting a strong New York flavor, it's not surprising that the board chose to acquire corporate office space in New

The Ensign 16-foot utility became the best-selling Gar Wood model of all time with 650 built over 18 months in two factories.

The Ensign 16-foot utilities were finished with gleaming white hull sides. A few had varnished hulls as this early example when suitable mahogany was available. *James Lane*

York City on the 20th floor of 342 Madison Avenue in June 1945. The New York trustees suggested that the New York design firm of Norman Bel Geddes be hired to design the new offices. Geddes recommended a suite of rooms with a reception and staff area, an office for the vice president, and an area for entertaining and meetings with a "clubroom" atmosphere.Glen Bassett said it was the company's goal to increase the boat division's sales to between $4 and $5 million per year. He further stated that it was his understanding that the boat division's sales had never exceeded $500,000 in any fiscal year. To increase sales to reach this projected goal, production might need to exceed the capacity of Marysville's facilities. He wanted the Geddes staff to evaluate the facilities as well as production methods. He also suggested that the Geddes Design firm develop one or two boats immediately and later on consider designs for the balance of the line. To his credit, Geddes was quick to say that he disagreed with this suggestion. He would prefer to study the boat operations as a whole first, then through analysis and research make specific recommendations where appropriate to improve the whole situation. The discussion finally narrowed itself down to a consideration of six hull sizes already drafted by the staff designers with a probable production of 4,000 units.

A meeting of this nature was unthinkable when Logan Wood and Gar Wood were in charge. Their ideas regarding boat production were always presented to the boat division first. They listened carefully to hear what their key employees could contribute before proceeding. They respected the opinions of the staff closest to the action because they knew what worked. If either of the Woods insisted on a new procedure, they were wise enough to step back and let their men figure out how to do it.

The new corporate executives were sitting in a Manhattan office building with bankers and artists, all unfamiliar with the boat division, making decisions about the new boat models. This marked the beginning of the unrealistic expectations to be placed upon the boat division. These decisions would come from corporate executives that knew little, and cared little, about the boat division's activities.

On Friday, June 29, 1945, Norman Bel Geddes and two of his associates, Sanford Johnson and J. G. Krueger, arrived in Detroit to meet with the Gar Wood executives prior to their initial visit to the boat factory on Saturday morning. During the afternoon meeting the nature of the Geddes service contract was reviewed along with the aspects of their permanent retainer arrangements. There were two possible approaches for establishing a working relationship

Another variation for the postwar models was the use of vinyl over plywood on the deck (left) rather than the traditional varnished mahogany planking (right).

One of the rarest postwar models is the 17-foot, 6-inch runabout. The shortage of mahogany forced Gar Wood to discontinue this model in favor of the more profitable 19-foot, 6-inch runabout. *Jim Rodgers*

with Gar Wood Industries and each was explained along with the associated costs involved. They agreed that Gar Wood Industries would retain the design firm for $25,000 per year for an overall study of all its divisions and would also pay for additional assignments. All additional assignments were to be estimated and approved in advance. The work on the boat division would be an additional assignment not covered by the retainer fee. Gar Wood Industries agreed to pay $40,270 in addition to the retainer fee to the design firm for the "boat division assignment." Their analysis of the boat division would include sketches, block models, renderings, plans, and a written report with their findings and recommendations. The initial contract with Norman Bel Geddes Associates was for $65,270, a considerable amount in 1945 dollars.

The afternoon meeting was followed by dinner and a two-hour evening meeting devoted to the boat division. It was at this Detroit meeting in which the Geddes people learned about the relationship and expectations that headquarters had for the boat division. The after-dinner session was surprisingly candid. Gar Wood executives described the boat division as "an industrial stepchild" that operated more like a small custom shop than a serious industry. They continued by saying that the boat division was, for many years, just an ego thing maintained by "the boss" to keep the popularity of the name "Gar Wood" alive, rather than to make a profit. More than one division chief felt that the boat division contributed little to the total enterprise. It was becoming abundantly clear to Geddes that his task would be more complex than simply suggesting new boat designs. The boat division had been protected for so long by Wood himself that the years of guardianship had created significant internal resentment.

The following morning the Geddes team traveled to the boat factory in Marysville. The meeting with the corporate executives caused Geddes some concern about what he would find at the boat factory. Ed Hancock and Jack Clifford were simply told that a New York firm would be visiting them to provide some ideas and discuss operations with them. During the visit they inspected the new prototype boats that had been developed as Gar Wood's entries for the postwar market. The real purpose of the Geddes visit was never clearly explained beforehand. It would prove to be an enlightening day for everyone involved.

The new experimental prototype models that the boat division designers had developed included a 15-foot utility; a 16-foot utility; a 16-foot, 6-inch utility; a 17-foot, 6-inch runabout; two versions of a 22-foot, 6-inch cabin utility; and a 26-foot express cruiser. These seven experimental boats were totally new concepts. There was no discernible lineage with

115

previous Gar Wood designs. They were wonderfully attractive and innovative designs that appeared to win solid approval from their enlightened guests. Each boat possessed enough modern features to be recognized as different, yet was still pleasing to those who were fond of traditional lines. The new boats were a complete break from the successful designs of Gar Wood's 1941 fleet.

Geddes was taken with the overall appearance of the prototypes. He observed, however, that they made little application of new materials developed during the war years, such as marine plywood, fiberglass, plastic, and vinyl. He acknowledged that the boats were pleasing to the eye and praised the staff for its accomplishments on these new prototypes. In his notes he affirmed the design achievement of the staff on the new boats, but added that he could see numerous places to incorporate modern materials to cut costs and improve on styling details.

As part of the analysis the Geddes designers wanted to know more about production methods, manufacturing costs, principal marketing areas, typical customer profiles, principal export nations, merchandising methods, and sources of supplies and materials. It was during this part of the visit that Hancock and others at the boat division began to sense that their visitors' relationship with Gar Wood Industries was more involved than they had been led to believe. They became more sensitive to the probing questions being

asked about boat division operations. Geddes sensed the shift in attitude. It seemed to be a prudent time to end this visit and plan another one in a few weeks.

After the initial meeting with Geddes and his staff, Hancock and Clifford knew that the working environment at Gar Wood Industries was changing. There would be greater scrutiny of the boat division's operations and the bottom line. From the time Wood began selling his common stock, they began to prepare themselves for increased pressure to raise profits. What surprised them was how quickly the board brought in outside consultants. Even more surprising was that they chose the tiny boat division, with its revolutionary factory, to be the first unit in the giant operation for review. Jack Clifford, known for his quick wit said, "It's a very good sign for us that after all these years the board of trustees was so interested in the boat division that they chose us to begin their efficiency study."

Within a few weeks Geddes' associates returned to Marysville for further study of the facilities and to interview as many of the workers as possible, including office staff, finishers, machinists, upholsterers, design staff, carpenters, and supervisors. They took several test runs in the new experimental models before they returned to New York to compile their recommendations.

The preliminary report cut right to the core of the boat division's posture on production and sales. The report was critical of the division's unorganized

The first 22-foot, 6-inch Sedan had a beautifully designed cabin enclosure. The cabin was too costly to build on the production models and had to be replaced with a less expensive version. *Gar Wood*

This unusual Overniter prototype model featured a raised deck, radical transom treatment, and a large open cockpit. It is believed this was the only one of this style built. *Gar Wood*

procedures that were more typical of a craft enterprise than a large manufacturing operation. It reported, "Their management never appears to know exactly how much money is made on each boat. They know that the profit realized on certain boats is sufficient to absorb the loss on others. The workers, in general, display skepticism toward the value of design services from an outside concern."

The Geddes report continued, observing that the boat division "needed to prove that they were more than stylists by demonstrating that they could contribute substantially to the Division's overall success. We encountered opposition to releasing engineering data and to allowing Geddes to make full scale drawings for boat designs." The report stated, "The Boat Division works directly from full size templates. The Gar Wood designers are also holding back on lines and offsets of boat hulls, taking a position that these are Gar Wood's stock in trade and should not be let out of the office. This attitude is explained by the Boat Division not knowing how long Geddes will be working for them and anticipating the possibility that some of the men working on the account might conceivably move on to one of their competitors."

It was apparent that the boat division was not a willing participant in using Geddes' services. They were reluctant to share valuable design details and methods of construction. They also were reluctant to provide accurate production data. When asked about their annual production volume, Hancock and Clifford were purposely vague and let the researchers believe that an average volume of 400 boats was "close." This sounded reasonable enough, but was much higher than the actual volume. During the 12 years of production from 1930 through 1941 in the Marysville factory, the highest volume year was in 1937. In that year a record high of 267 boats were built. The average volume in Marysville was only 138 boats a year. The distrust for the consultants became so strong that the boat division managers were unwilling to provide accurate data to their consultants if they believed the information might be used to hurt them.

There was growing distrust between the boat division and the consultants as it became clear their priorities differed. The Geddes report went on to say that "the basic attitude of the Division's management in regard to their product is that they wish to produce the best quality boats with the highest possible speed, and to give these boats as much appearance value as possible but, paradoxically, they disregard that these boats must be priced competitively."

The report found the boat division's attitude toward price competition was most unusual for an industrial organization. It was believed to be the result of a conviction that Gar Wood always builds the best and fastest boats, but at a price. The consultants also believed that operating this way would prevent real financial success. The early analysis was "the boat plant is basically nothing more than a large, overgrown boat shop. It's a shop where boats are made, not produced." The report got even more critical, stating, "New materials and innovative methods that are not part of boat building tradition, are regarded skeptically and without any imagination. There is an over emphasis on tradition and craftsmanship that keeps prices too high."

Geddes believed that in order for the boat division to ever become profitable it needed to increase its production significantly to 1,000 units a year and, perhaps, more. He believed that the Marysville factory was only suitable to build a maximum of 500 boats annually. His study showed that expansion at Marysville was not practical because the land was leased and not owned by Gar Wood. He suggested that a second boat facility was needed. The tank division was also in need of new facilities and the company should consider sharing space with another division. In late 1945 Bergen decided to acquire the former Dodge boat factory in Newport News, Virginia. It was a large facility and ideal for both the tank division and the boat division together. It would provide Gar Wood Industries with an East Coast location that placed both divisions closer to their customers. A deal was struck with Dodge, and plans began immediately to get Newport News ready to build boats and tanks.

The acquisition of the Dodge factory set in motion Gar Wood Industries' plans to build a new boat factory 800 miles from Marysville. The change from war boats to peacetime boats had already taxed Hancock and Clifford, and now more sweeping changes were at hand. Hiring and training new staff and maintaining quality in the new facility was a daunting proposition. For Hancock and Clifford it was too much change too fast, made worse by the fact that those now calling the shots were far removed from the day-to-day job of building the boating industry's finest craft.

It was decided that the Newport News factory would begin by concentrating its efforts in building the 16-foot utility exclusively. This made sense because this boat was the easiest model in the line to build. It was also better suited to the Newport News facilities. After becoming established, it was thought that other models could be built in Newport News. For now, the task was to build as many 16-foot Ensigns as possible.

For the employees of the Gar Wood Boat division, this was an unnecessarily difficult period. They had successfully fulfilled their defense contracts for both the Army and Navy. They had a head start on new designs and had developed their largest and strongest dealer network ever. The Gar Wood design staff had created a superb line of postwar models. They planned on three lengths of utility boats, two lengths of runabouts, and a new, small cruiser.

The postwar version of the Overniter was highly anticipated, but it proved to be more expensive than the limited market for small cruisers could afford. *Gar Wood*

The 16-foot Ensign utility was fast and nimble. Its modest price and modern design attracted many new dealers into Gar Wood's postwar organization. The Ensign was Gar Wood's volume leader. *Mystic Seaport, Rosenfeld Collection, Mystic, Connecticut*

The 16-foot utility model, called the Ensign, would be the low-priced entry designed with a reverse sheer, slightly barrel bow, white painted sides, runabout style windshield, and all-vinyl interior. It would have three engine options starting with a four-cylinder, 61-horsepower Kermath Jeep at 31 miles per hour to the six-cylinder, 115-horsepower Chrysler Crown at 38 miles per hour. This was a model that every dealer could afford to have on display throughout the year. With the Chrysler Crown option at $2,055, it would provide exhilarating speeds for six passengers. Some models used plywood decks covered with vinyl that were quite attractive in an effort to conserve on scarce mahogany.

The 18-foot, 6-inch utility model, called the Cavalier, had runabout styling, a full barrel bow, reverse sheer, attractive runabout windshield, rakish cutwater flared at the top, and seating for six with speeds to 37 miles per hour. It would also be offered in a nicely styled hardtop version called the Royale. This version used a wood-framed wind-

shield to provide adequate headroom inside the sheltered area. Both models offered three engine options from 93 horsepower to 140 horsepower with a maximum speed of 37 miles per hour. Prices started at $2,395 for the open model and $2,770 for the sedan model.

The 22-foot, 6-inch model, called the Diplomat, was a full-size craft with 7-foot, 6-inch beam and a three-section windshield. Reverse sheer, barrel bow, and full rounding of the transom into the top of the aft deck created a beautifully sculptured hull that was unmatched by any stock utility. It featured seats for nine passengers and speeds to 32 miles per hour with a Chrysler Royal. The hardtop version, called the Ambassador, required three styling changes to the cabin design before the final configuration was achieved. The initial cabin design was similar to the 22-foot Chris-Craft Sedan utility where the windshield and the roof flowed together smoothly. The next version had a smart metal-framed windshield and beautiful cabin with flowing side panels that swept to the aft deck. Both of these versions were too expensive and too labor intensive to construct. The final version was the hardtop style with open sides that provided a feeling of openness with the protection of a permanent roof, ventilating windshields, and removable side curtains. The price for the 22-foot, 6-inch utility was $6,000, and the sedan hard top was $6,800.

The design staff initially planned on four runabouts, but dropped the larger two in favor of the 17-foot, 6-inch and 19-foot, 6-inch models.

The 17-foot, 6-inch runabout was intended to provide a fast, flashy boat to compete with Chris-Craft's 17-foot Deluxe Runabout, the Century Sea Maid, and the Higgins 17-foot sport utility. Its generous beam and freeboard gave it the appearance of a longer, larger boat. It provided seating for six, and with the 140-horsepower Gray Fireball it was rated at better than 40 miles per hour. It was an excellent design, but dealers and customers preferred to spend the extra money to have the 19-foot, 6-inch model, so it was dropped from production after just 12 models were produced. The 17-foot, 6-inch runabout was designed to sell for $2,400.

The 19-foot, 6-inch runabout called the Commodore was the style setter of the Gar Wood fleet with many innovations, including barrel bow and stern, deck rails fore and aft, split cutwater, reverse sheer, rounded covering boards, windshield bracket air scoops, and magnificent overall good looks. The swept-up water line made a continuous curve with the cutwater that was very stylish. The barrel bow was similar to the design of the 1941 Chris-Craft custom runabout that in all likelihood inspired the Gar Wood design. It was surprising that Chris-Craft abandoned this feature in its postwar custom runabout. Gar Wood's runabout had two engine options: the 115-horsepower Chrysler Crown at $3,475 with speeds to 36 miles per hour and the Gray 140-horsepower Fireball at $3,825 rated at 38 miles per hour. Early models used vinyl very effectively to cover the curved covering boards.

One of the earliest postwar prototype models was the 25-foot, 11-inch Overniter. Gar Wood's staff knew that a small, sporty cruiser would be popular in the postwar market. Marine industry studies had shown a definite trend toward small, affordable cruisers before the war. The original, prewar Overniters were superb designs, but did not offer enough interior room for most buyers. The new Overniter was offered in two versions, an Express model that slept two and the four-sleeper Sedan Cruiser. Both models were offered with a pair of Chrysler Crowns for speeds over 30 miles per hour.

The Sedan Cruiser was priced at $11,500.

Early documents indicated that they planned to offer two more runabouts, the 22-foot, 6-inch rear engine Streamliner and a new 27-foot, 6-inch triple cockpit model. No renderings of these boats have ever been located, indicating that they were probably never fully designed and were simply ideas. They were listed, however, in the 1946 Boat Show Issue of *Motor Boating* as part of Gar Wood's 1946 fleet. There are no factory photos of either of these boats and no hull number assignments in the company ledger.

Each model was given a distinct name, carrying over the practice from the 1941 Gar Wood Trophy Fleet. On the 1941 models these model names were hand lettered in script and located on the hull just above the chine near the cutwater. Some of the same names were repeated for the postwar boats but not necessarily on the same models.

The stunning postwar models were a total departure from the traditional Gar Wood Boats that had immediately preceded them, and people began to speculate that the new designs came from Norman Bel Geddes. In fact all of these new designs were done by Gar Wood's in-house design staff, and most of them were being constructed and water tested months before Geddes was under contract with Gar Wood. Geddes inspected the experimental prototype models on June 30, 1945, when he made his first visit to the Marysville factory. By September Geddes' design staff reported that they should leave "all (new) boats (exactly) as planned by Gar Wood Industries for 1946–47. Exclude everything pertaining to hull design unless it is an obvious contribution." The team of design assistants led by Ed Kaunitz, who trained under George Joachim, were the men actually responsible for all the new postwar designs. Early photographs taken by Ed Hancock confirm that all the postwar designs were completed long before Geddes was under contract.

Still, Geddes began to get credit for Gar Wood's new designs. In May 1945 the first illustrated ads for Gar Wood began to appear in the boating magazines showing the new barrel bow treatment with the split cutwater top and the anchor design forward chocks. The official news release was dated November 7, 1945. Weston Smith's notice in *Financial World* reported, "The new line of pleasure motorboats to be introduced by Gar Wood Industries will be the last word in streamlining—Norman Bel Geddes, industrial designer, has been engaged to re-style several models for postwar introduction."

An early news release from Gar Wood president Glen Bassett, on October 20, 1945, stated, "Norman

Bel Geddes, noted industrial designer, has been retained to re-style its entire varied line of products, with special emphasis on its postwar motorboats. This is believed to be the first time that modern industrial design will be applied to such products as bulldozers and dump trucks of which the company is a leading producer."

By mid-1946 Gar Wood advertisements began to use phrases with the words *styled by Norman Bel Geddes*. By January 1947 the words grew to read *styled on the ever-inspired drawing board of Norman Bel Geddes*. Geddes' name was added to all the promotional material to gain a measure of prestige for the superb designs, whose true creators were staff designers, including Ed Kaunitz, Jim Drake, and Ed Rogoski.

Part of the reason Geddes' name came to be attached to the new designs was that their features were so different from Gar Wood's prior craft. The barrel bow feature, the new rolled monkey rails, and the Gar Wood anchor trim were announced in March 1945. In May a photo ad pointed out the "flowing line" design and war-developed sound insulation of the exquisite 22-foot, 6-inch cabin utility. The next issue of *Rudder* magazine featured photos of the 15-foot utility (this experimental model preceded the 16-foot utility); the 19-foot, 6-inch runabout; and the 22-foot, 6-inch cabin utility. All of the photos showed the boats running. In order for ads to appear in magazines, the copy material had to be in the hands of the publisher several weeks ahead of the actual printing and distribution dates, which again confirms the fact that these new Gar Wood designs were all prepared and completed before Geddes entered the picture.

Gar Wood Boats had established a system of evolutionary change from one year to the next. Rarely was a new model introduced that did not closely resemble a model from the previous year. This continuity fostered recognition of traditional Gar Wood designs. The war broke Gar Wood's production continuity and brought different ideas to the drawing

The 18-foot, 6-inch utility adapted well to the new open-style sedan hardtop design that provided abundant ventilation and excellent visibility. This top was a practical solution to lower production costs. *Mystic Seaport, Rosenfeld Collection, Mystic, Connecticut*

The sedan version of the 22-foot, 6-inch utility featured an attractive hardtop design that influenced Chris-Craft to develop a similar style top for their Continental series. *Mystic Seaport, Rosenfeld Collection, Mystic, Connecticut*

board. Many Gar Wood enthusiasts still wonder why the boat division abandoned every model from its outstanding 1941 designs to start all over. There is evidence that the designers planned to include the 22-foot, 6-inch Streamliner and a 27-foot, 6-inch triple-cockpit runabout from their previous designs, but neither of these boats actually materialized among the postwar models.

During the quiet period that followed the Navy's termination of its contracts in early 1944, Gar Wood's design staff had time to develop new, experimental designs. They could do this with little competitive pressure because other boatbuilders were still fulfilling their defense contracts. They wanted to deliver truly modern craft to the ardent boaters who had set their sport aside during the war years. Gar Wood believed that postwar boats should be a new generation of expression. There were rumors that Higgins, which planned to enter the small boat market, had several attractive and modern designs using plywood construction and super smooth automotive finishes.

Chris-Craft was still Gar Wood's major rival in the field of runabouts, utilities, and cabin utilities, and each firm always had a good idea what the other was planning. Chris-Craft chose not to go for all-new styles for its first postwar line and instead updated its prewar designs. The decision allowed Chris-Craft to bring its prewar forms and jigs out of storage and begin production immediately. By adding a distinctive bow cap feature, modifying the stem, and adding a few new styling details, Chris-Craft brought out its new line of boats more rapidly than their competition. Their only totally new model was the 20-foot custom runabout. This boat introduced the blond mahogany deck trim feature that would be the company's special feature for the next decade. With more

buyers than available boats, Chris-Craft's decision to simply update its prewar models turned out to be a wise one.

In terms of pure design, Gar Wood's new models were the most advanced and tastefully modern boats offered in the field. The 16-inch Ensign utility was an interesting blend of both a runabout and a utility. It had a barrel bow, sporty runabout-style windshield, and reverse sheer, which provided increased depth to this small boat. Even the prototype of this model had white painted sides, which gave the boat a uniquely attractive appearance. On the practical side, the white hull permitted the extensive use of North American cedar during a time when all boatbuilders were hindered by the lack of high-quality mahogany. With the six-cylinder engine options, the Ensign was a thrilling boat that would level out and plane like a Speedster.

One short-lived styling decision on the Ensign models was the use of vinyl to cover plywood on the fore and aft decks in order to cut time and reduce costs. The monkey rails and covering boards would still be varnished mahogany. This idea helped conserve on scarce mahogany. This treatment was tried for a short time in January 1946 on the Ensigns built at the Marysville factory. The dealers preferred the traditional mahogany planked varnished decks, and the use of vinyl on the decks was discontinued.

In February 1946 Gar Wood experienced its first labor strike at the boat factory. It didn't last long, and there were no picket lines to prevent clerical staff and engineers from going to work. The labor strikes at Chris-Craft were far more serious and often involved hostile confrontations. When Chris-Craft workers were on strike, some of their better finishers would make the short trip to Marysville and join their neighbors at the Gar Wood plant as daily workers. The Chris-Craft workers were highly skilled and always welcomed at Gar Wood. Bill Wright, a former Gar Wood design engineer said, "Chris-Craft had a superb hull finishing crew which was an asset to our production during their strikes. Good hull finishers were always in great demand."

The standard finish for the Ensign was white hull sides, red waterline stripe, bronze bottom paint, varnished decks, and transom. The interior was royal blue and gray vinyl. In a few instances when there was enough matched mahogany the entire boat would be varnished. The Ensign was intended to be a boat that anyone who wanted a small all-purpose boat could afford. It was also designed to make it easier for dealers to keep new boats in stock and on display. Jack Clifford's position was that their dealers needed to have a new Gar Wood in their inventory all the time, and this model was perfect for that purpose. With its white hull and all-vinyl interior, this was as close to a low-maintenance craft as there was on the market. It was with this boat that Gar Wood planned to build its new, vast dealer network, and it was believed it would be the company's key to future success. The boat was a hit with their dealers and customers and was one of the best-selling boats of the early postwar period.

This remarkable little craft had many special features that were rarely found in a boatbuilder's least expensive model. The reverse sheer design, made popular by Elco's PT boats, enabled this small boat to have generous freeboard without looking stubby. The sides were only modestly flared providing more width at the waterline. The runabout-styled windshield enhanced the sporty appearance, and the white hull accentuated the reverse sheer and barrel bow. Even the flared water-line added a sporty touch to this outstanding boat. Owners lucky enough to get an Ensign with a 115-horsepower Chrysler Crown were in for blazing performance. This model was the first small utility with muscle power and a level of performance not soon forgotten. At $1,930, it was priced in range with the competition.

The small runabout of the postwar Gar Wood fleet was the 17-foot, 6-inch model. It was beautifully styled with rounded covering boards, barrel bow, barrel stern speeds over 40 miles per hour, and all-mahogany finish. It was designed to compete directly with Chris-Craft's 17-foot deluxe runabout. Yet it was too close in size to Gar Wood's 19-foot, 6-inch Commodore runabout, which could command a much higher price. With scarcity of good mahogany becoming a growing concern, this model was temporarily discontinued in favor of the larger runabout. The few that have survived (three are known to exist) are among the rarest of all Gar Wood models since only 12 17-foot, 6-inch runabouts were built.

The 19-foot, 6-inch Commodore was the most beautiful twin cockpit runabout of its time, maybe of all time. Its cut water split into wings that blended into the rub rails, exposing a mass of mahogany that curved into the stem. This barrel bow was crowned with the attractive deck anchor whose flukes emerged as chocks. The covering boards were fully rounded over the length of the boat. The upper section of the transom rounds off completely into the hull sides eliminating any trace of a traditional upper corner where the hull side, deck, and transom meet. The side windshield brackets are sculpted into attractive, functional ventilators. The fore and aft decks have streamlined safety rails over their full length. The Commodore is breathtaking, stylish, modern, and yet, still traditional. The boat is a masterpiece.

With cost a driving consideration, the elegant Commodore was soon simplified. The streamlined ventilators on the side windshield brackets, the deck rails fore and aft, and the bow anchor soon disappeared. The rounded covering boards gave way to

The 19-foot, 6-inch Commodore shows excellent high-speed performance with six passengers onboard. With its beautifully sculptured hull and flowing curves, many consider this to be the most attractive runabout under 20 feet. *Mystic Seaport, Rosenfeld Collection, Mystic, Connecticut*

more conventional style covering boards, and the radical stern rounding became less dramatic.

The 18-foot, 6-inch all-varnish mahogany utility was a fast, attractive model that had nice features such as runabout windshield, reverse sheer, barrel bow, rounded monkey rails, and split cut water. The unique sedan version had a hardtop that was open on the sides, giving shelter without being confining. This type of top was very cool on hot days and snug during inclement weather with the snap-in side curtains. The top enhanced the appearance of this attractive boat with its clean simple lines that flowed from the special windshield to the aft part of the cockpit. Once again Gar Wood offered the most attractive sedans in the business.

The 22-foot, 6-inch utility was a big boat, with more beam and more freeboard than its rival, the popular Chris-Craft 22-foot Sportsman. It had more flare and more crown on the deck than the Chris-Craft, and it was heavier. The Gar Wood had a superbly rounded aft deck and transom as well as a barrel bow. It sported an unusual three-section windshield and had a price of $6,000 with a Chrysler Royal 8 that drove it 32 miles per hour. The sedan version had three different top designs in an attempt to reduce the price of the sedan version. The final version used an open-style top similar to the 18-foot, 6-inch sedan rather than the more deluxe cabin enclosures with sliding glass windows. The sedan model with the open-style top sold for $6,800, which was in the price range of many family cruisers from other builders.

The 25-foot, 11-inch Overniter was the flagship of the postwar Gar Wood fleet in both size and price. This large hull was part of the same bloodline as all the other postwar Gar Woods with its barrel bow, split cutwater, and reverse sheer. It was a major departure from the previous Overniters. This boat was a cruiser that slept four, offered a popular dinette, and had twin engines that gave the boat

Industrial designer Norman Bel Geddes created exciting full-color advertisements to provide Gar Wood Boats with a more contemporary image to attract younger new buyers.

speeds more than 30 miles per hour. This boat was not like any other 26-foot family cruiser of its day because of its special styling that indicated a heritage with speedboat origins.

The Gar Wood Boat division had a good start for the postwar market. The new designs were outstanding and were prepared well in advance of many other builders. If there had been a boat show in 1946, Gar Wood Boats would have made the strongest statement on the features of new design.

Gar Wood was present in January 1947 for the first postwar New York boat show. By this time the Geddes' influence over the Gar Wood executives was powerful. Geddes stuck to his belief that Gar Wood could reduce costs by extensive use of modern synthetic materials. He was very persuasive, and he sold the executives on the idea that painted hulls would be more attractive to postwar buyers than far more costly varnished hulls that were a throwback to the past. He pointed to the new Higgins as the boat manufacturer that understood the postwar buyer better than any other company. Higgins was ahead of everyone in using modern marine plywood and applying fast-drying, high-gloss, sprayed-on automotive finishes. Their lightweight hulls were faster with less horsepower and were easier to produce. Geddes convinced the top executives that they needed to be more modern, more like Higgins. He pointed out that even traditional firms like Richardson made radical changes in design using modern molded plywood and eliminating varnished wood entirely.

Geddes then presented a spectacular, full-color, full-page layout for a display ad. It featured the new Commodore runabout with a black-painted hull and white deck on a blue background. The boat was headed right at the viewer. The driver looked like Gene Kelly, the actor, with three gorgeous girls aboard. Everyone was smiling and having a great time. It was an impressive layout that had strong appeal. Everyone in the boardroom loved it.

By this time Edwin Hancock didn't need a picture to see that the boat division was no longer in his control. After 20 years of guiding the destiny of the famous Gar Wood Boat division, Hancock retired in 1946. The corporate changes were more than he could handle, and the Geddes influence was becoming so destructive to what he stood for, he could see no possible way to survive. In October 1946, Robert Lawson, a corporate administrator, was appointed manager of the boat division.

In December 1946 new hulls are stacked up in anticipation of a labor strike at the Marysville factory. In three months boat production ended permanently. *Bill Wright*

Geddes' full-page color ad of the black-and-white 19-foot, 6-inch runabout appeared in several major magazines prior to the 1947 New York boat show and created quite a stir among the competition. The ad was a superb illustration that will always be remembered as Gar Wood's most creative ad.

On the advice of the expensive design consultants, Gar Wood's officers decided they should present this new image at the 1947 boat show. Each of their four display models for the show would be completely painted. There would be no varnished surfaces except for transoms. The 16-foot Ensign was all white. The 19-foot, 6-inch Commodore's hull was black with a white deck. The 18-foot, 6-inch utility was dark red. The forth model in the show was the 22-foot, 6-inch sedan in royal blue. Rather than looking sheik and appealing, the boats disappointed boat show visitors, who looked forward to the famous Gar Wood varnish mahogany. Before long, rumors started at the show that Gar Wood's painted hulls were a last-minute decision "cover up" of poor workmanship and inferior wood mahogany that could not be varnished attractively. The public reaction to the Gar Wood display was a nightmare for Jack Clifford. He knew Gar Wood had the best designed small craft in the show, and the consultant's decision to cover them with paint turned out to be an error of such magnitude that it would turn dealers and customers away. It was a strategic mistake from which recovery would be difficult. Clifford knew it was time to leave.

Ed Hancock and Jack Clifford had done a remarkable job getting the boat factory converted from defense production to totally new pleasure boat designs. Pleasure boats, built for style, comfort, and recreation, required many different techniques and quality standards than sturdy, stripped-down, war boats. Former employees returned from the military looking forward to building pleasure boats again. A lot of retraining was required with new materials, new methods, and new designs. The building lumber after the war was not of the same quality the woodworkers were used to. Often they were required to substitute woods such as cedar for mahogany for bottom planking. Vinyl upholstery replaced leather upholstery. Interior ceilings were now sheets of plywood covered with vinyl. Materials were in short supply so that incomplete boats were stacked up waiting for missing items. The factory in Newport News needed attention almost daily. Marine engines were always in short supply because the manufacturers had to take care of the demands of the auto industry first.

Even with all of these problems Gar Wood managed to build more boats in the 14 months from February 1946 to April 1947 than at any time in the company's history. Nearly 900 Gar Woods were built in the most difficult times with conversions, shortages, expansion, and a strike. This was five times the volume of 1941. Surely another year without all of the problems faced in the immediate postwar period would show even greater increases in production.

But it was not to be. Gar Wood Boats, which had produced many of the most beautiful and best-performing watercraft of its day, ceased production in April 1947. Having survived the Depression, contributed to World War II, and returned with great fanfare and expectations, the boat division fell victim to the new priorities of its corporate keepers.

The employees of the boat division were called together when the decision to close down boat production was announced, and those wishing to work with other Gar Wood divisions were given the opportunity. It was described as a necessary "business decision" by Glen Bassett, corporation president. For many of the veteran boatbuilders they simply called it "payback time," and a wonderful era of boatbuilding ended.

Looking for a logical reason why Gar Wood Industries abruptly ended boat production when it seemed to have the right models, the production volume, and the dealer network necessary to succeed is not simple. There are many theories. Many who were close to the company at this time felt that there was long-standing internal resentment toward the boat division. For more than 20 years Wood protected the boat operations from any corporate criticism. Overworked corporate executives were silently aware of vast sums of corporate profits being spent to build world-class race boats for Wood's personal gratification. Wood expected much of his executives, but paid them modestly at best. Long after the racing competition ended, Wood still looked out for the boat factory even after it became a corporate division. Boat division losses were absorbed by other divisions that did not enjoy the same privilege. When Wood finally divested himself completely, it was time for the executives who had endured years of watching this special treatment to exact their revenge on the boat division.

It was of little consequence that Gar Wood Boats were considered some of the finest examples of their type in the world. The ax fell shortly after the board retained Norman Bel Geddes. Right from the start he was at odds with the boat division and their traditional craft shop mentality. They were uncooperative with Geddes, withholding data from his staff and scoffing at his people's suggestions to modernize. The corporate enemies of the boat division watched with delight as Geddes reported to the executives details of their primitive style and suggested impossible boat production goals in the absence of boat division management.

The opening of the Newport News factory was largely to facilitate the necessary expansion of the highly profitable truck tank body division. Building boats in the same facility was a token attempt to provide additional production space that was given little corporate support. When Ed Hancock and Jack Clifford resigned it was the end of an era, and closing the division was just a matter of time. The boat division could never meet the new corporate standards for profitability and efficiency. Closing the boat division down was a concealed internal goal for many years waiting for an opportunity.

Gar Wood left a legacy of great boats that may never be equaled. All were carefully constructed of superior materials to perform properly at a wide range of speeds. There was never a Gar Wood Boat that was anything but a superb example of the art of boatbuilding. Owning a Gar Wood Boat is a wonderful experience that only a few hundred fortunate people can enjoy. Gar Wood Boats have become one of the most sought-after collectibles in the world of classic boating. At boat shows they always seem to draw the largest crowds. We are fortunate that Gar Wood's interest in boats provided the opportunity for a group of talented craftsmen to create fine boats for a quarter of a century. Gar Wood's personal wealth and interest maintained production long after this level of quality became hard to justify in the boat business. By all rights, Gar Wood should have closed its doors in 1933. Every boat built by the company after that terrible Depression year is a gift to the boating world from a man who put quality and his love of boats ahead of profits.

From 1922 until 1947 there were some 3,300 Gar Wood Boats built. Of this number it is estimated that about 500 Gar Woods have survived. Most of these are now in good hands and should be enjoyed for years to come. Six superb Gar Woods are on display in the Antique Boat Museum in Clayton, New York.

Even the final fleet of Gar Wood designs representing a new beginning were every bit as original and distinctive as the lineage that preceded them. Gar Wood Boats were superb to the end; never cheapened, never compromised, and always the smartest looking and finest performing boats among their contemporaries. After surviving the perilous Depression, it's ironic that the boat division's demise occurred in the year of their greatest production. In its final year, the factory built five times more vessels than its annual average volume.

There has never been another boatbuilding firm like Gar Wood. For 25 years Gar Wood designed and built the finest boats of its time. The staff was skilled, fiercely proud of their work, and extremely loyal. They enjoyed being part of a small company with a worldwide reputation of excellence. Employees were never asked to compromise on quality or performance to keep costs lower. A customer could select from a wide range of stock models or have a custom boat built.

Owning a Gar Wood Boat was a symbol of discriminating good taste then as it still is today for contemporary owners. The surviving Gar Woods have become the most desirable classic boats because their design and overall styling are recognized as the best of their day. Their ride and performance are superior to all the boats of their era and equal to or better than many modern craft.

There have been attempts to recreate Gar Wood Boats by contemporary builders. No one has done a better job than the Turcotte Brothers in upstate New York. Turcotte Brothers had the full range of skills and all the passion to succeed. The company produced 60 superb recreations of Gar Wood's best designs. What the company didn't have was Gar Wood's unlimited wealth, which is what it took to keep all the elements together during difficult times.

Gar Wood Boats represent the best of the golden era of classic boating.

Marysville, Michigan, was proud to be the home of Gar Wood Boats. Large billboards on every road to Marysville gave vivid testimony to the company's noble status.

Index